Leadership and Governance in Primary Healthcare

Good leadership and governance at all levels of the healthcare system are necessary for better performance of the system and health outcomes. A lack of good leadership and governance practices can lead to the misuse of health system inputs such as human resources, health commodities and financial resources, hence lowering the quality of services delivered. Thus, this practical handbook was developed through collaborative efforts to respond to the need to improve good governance practices at the primary healthcare level in resource-limited healthcare systems.

Key Features:

- Improves the management of primary health facilities.
- Helps the health facility managers and teams at the primary healthcare level to effectively and efficiently lead and manage facilities.
- Enumerates practical scenarios on health issues that commonly occur in health facilities and provides alternative ways of addressing the issues raised in these scenarios.

Leadership and Governance in Primary Healthcare

An Exemplar for Practice in Resource Limited Settings

Edited by

Mackfallen G. Anasel
Senior Lecturer and Researcher
Department of Health Systems Management,
School of Public Administration and Management, Mzumbe University, Tanzania

Ntuli A. Kapologwe
Director of Health, Social Welfare and Nutrition Services at the
President's Office Regional Administration and
Local Government, Tanzania

Albino Kalolo
Senior Lecturer and Researcher
Department of Public Health, Faculty of Medicine
St. Francis University College of Health and Allied Sciences,
Ifakara, Tanzania

CRC Press
Taylor & Francis Group
Boca Raton   London   New York

CRC Press is an imprint of the
Taylor & Francis Group, an **informa** business

First edition published 2023
by CRC Press
6000 Broken Sound Parkway NW, Suite 300, Boca Raton, FL 33487–2742

and by CRC Press
4 Park Square, Milton Park, Abingdon, Oxon, OX14 4RN

CRC Press is an imprint of Taylor & Francis Group, LLC

ISBN: 978-1-032-38799-4 (hbk)
ISBN: 978-1-032-38796-3 (pbk)
ISBN: 978-1-003-34682-1 (ebk)

DOI: 10.1201/9781003346821

Typeset in Times
by Apex CoVantage, LLC

Contents

Foreword

Tanzania is a pioneer in primary healthcare. Since 1961, Tanzania has been implementing health policies to achieve primary healthcare for all. These policies were decades in advance of the 1978 World Health Organization's landmark Alma Ata *Declaration of Health for All,* based on primary healthcare. By 1978, Tanzania had already built and staffed a health services infrastructure placing a staffed primary care health facility within 5 km of 90% of its largely rural population—a remarkable achievement unmatched anywhere else in Africa at the time. The basic, well-tested architecture of the Tanzanian health system remains fundamentally the same today, with its hierarchy of at least one regional hospital at the regional level, at least one district hospital at the district level, one health center at the division level and one dispensary at the ward level, matching the administrative governance structures of the county.

In the mid-1980s, I had the privilege of working with the Tanzania Ministry of Health and witnessing the early years of this endeavor. At that time, the Primary Health Care Unit in the Ministry of Health was led by Dr Faustin Magari, working out of a closet-sized office in the Ministry's headquarters along Samora Avenue Street in Dar es Salaam. In those days, Tanzanian primary healthcare efforts were focused on exploring the use of community health workers supporting the communities in the catchment areas of their nearest dispensary. These lightly trained community health workers were intended to bring the most commonly needed primary healthcare curative services beyond the district level to the village or community level, providing accessible care while taking some of the load off of dispensaries for the most common, easily treated conditions.

In the meantime, a global debate developed among international health development partners fearing that the original ideals of Alma Ata for "comprehensive primary healthcare", with its strong emphasis on community participation and intersectoral collaboration and characterized by a continuum of promotive, preventive, rehabilitative and curative services to sustainably address underlying causes of ill health, would be too slow, costly and impractical. Donor attention was diverted away from comprehensive primary healthcare and instead, development partners invested heavily in primary healthcare focused on "selective primary healthcare" with the intention of more rapid interim gains based on professional technical inputs for selected curative and preventive health services such as immunization, growth monitoring and oral rehydration. As a result, efforts directed at less qualified community health worker services came to an end in Tanzania and a disease-driven, rather than health-driven, prioritization in the health sector emerged and prevailed for many years.

Fast forward 35 years to today, and a wealth of experience in managing the complex and evolving primary healthcare scene in Tanzania has accrued. In this interval, the whole context of the health sector has evolved. Decentralization has been more carefully executed. Health system definitions and frameworks, such as the six building blocks, have been widely adopted. New metrics for the burden of disease have been developed and applied. A new appreciation of the relative cost-effectiveness of interventions and strategies has improved resource allocation and the efficiency of health services. Major global investments have been addressing selected high-burden diseases such as HIV/AIDS, tuberculosis and malaria for highly cost-effective immunization. Most importantly, child mortality has been reduced by over 70%, and overall life expectancy in Tanzania has improved dramatically. Today, there is a movement back toward more comprehensive primary healthcare approaches under the umbrella of health systems for universal health coverage.

Nevertheless, problems and questions remain. How best can primary healthcare be integrated into the health system still dominated by the disease approach, especially given the rising ratio of chronic, non-communicable disease to declining communicable disease rates? How best can primary healthcare be managed within rapidly changing complex adaptive systems such as the health system which, in turn, is embedded in the wider, ever-changing socio-political-economic systems of which it is a part? How best can system-wide thinking be applied to the prevailing framework of the health system? There has been well-documented attention, investments and progress across most of the health system framework's building blocks, especially health services, health financing, health informatics, medicines and technologies and, to some extent, in health human resources, but virtually no progress in the governance of health systems.

This handbook, edited by Anasel, Kapologwe and Kalolo, puts a much-needed focus on practical leadership and governance issues for primary healthcare in Tanzania. It is based on contemporary, real-world scenarios and lessons from the front lines. The scenarios chosen as worked examples are fascinating and vexing governance problems faced by communities, health workers, managers and other stakeholders. Important in the authors' approach is that they have gone far beyond the Governance building block of health systems to unpack governance issues as they play out in each of the other five health building block sub-systems of health service delivery, workforce, information

systems, commodities and technologies and financing and financial management. In addition to the rich description and systems analysis of the scenarios, the authors complete the story for each scenario with guidance on how to
shape an action plan to resolve the issues.

This handbook is a welcome approach given that so much of the literature
on governance in health systems has been abstract, academic and theoretical.
Reflecting on the primary healthcare efforts of the '80s in Tanzania, I recall
that in every dispensary there were well-worn, practical handbooks on the
shelf such as *Mahali Pasipo na Daktari* (Where there is no Doctor) and other
practical guides and handbooks for community health and community health
workers at the primary care level. It is high time that such a handbook for the
governance of primary healthcare is now available as an essential resource to
front-line managers and management teams.

Don de Savigny
Professor of Health Systems and Policies
Swiss Tropical and Public Health Institute

Preface

Leadership and governance at all levels of the healthcare system are cornerstones for improved system performance and health outcomes. When leadership and governance structures operate optimally, often there are gains such as effective, accountable, responsive, high-quality and inclusive health service delivery to the population. Lack of good leadership and governance practices instead can lead to misuse of health system inputs such as human resources, infrastructures, health commodities and financial resources, hence lowering the quality of services delivered. Thus, this handbook was developed through collaborative efforts envisioned to respond to the needs of improving leadership and governance practices at the primary healthcare level in the Tanzanian healthcare system.

This handbook is a first edition geared to improve the management of primary health facilities in Tanzania. This handbook's objective is to improve the ability of primary healthcare facility managers and management teams, as well as to assist them in leading and managing the facilities in an effective and efficient manner. The handbook provides a practical guide and scenarios regarding health issues that commonly occur in health facilities, along with alternative ways of addressing them.

This practical handbook provides various methods that can be used to improve the performance of health facilities. Therefore, it has been developed to reflect the six World Health Organization (WHO) health system building blocks, namely, management of health facilities, service delivery, health workforce, health information systems, health commodities and technologies, and health financing and financial management.

This handbook highlights the ongoing government initiatives to enhance Tanzanians' health status and develop the country's health systems by fostering good governance and leadership in primary healthcare and beyond. Therefore, the Ministry of Health (MoH) and the President's Office—Regional Administration and Local Government (PO-RALG) urge all health facility in-charges and management teams to use this practical guide consistently. The handbook is envisaged to serve as a quick, day-to-day reference for leading and managing all facility operations such as planning, budgeting, implementation, monitoring and evaluation processes.

The readers will find this handbook useful in leadership and governance that respond to the needs of improving good governance practices at the primary healthcare level, especially in resource-limited countries. We hope this handbook will stimulate practitioners, students and researchers to study these examples and come up with new ones for others to learn.

We would like to express our gratitude to all of the authors who contributed chapters to this handbook, as well as to the publishers for all of their support throughout the entire publishing process. We want to express our sincere gratitude to Himani Dwivedi and Shivangi Pramanik in particular for their tireless efforts, persistent reminders and patience with us during the editing process.

Acknowledgments

The successful development of this handbook is a tribute of individuals and institutions who committed their valuable time and resources. MoH and PO-RALG appreciate the technical and financial support that facilitated the development of this book.

Specific acknowledgment is extended to the officials from the MoH and PO-RALG for spearheading and facilitating the development of this book. Special gratitude is extended to the honorable Dr. Dorothy O. Gwajima—Minister for Community Development, Women and Special Group, who was the then Deputy Permanent Secretary (PO-RALG—Health), for her leadership and guidance that led to the development of this handbook.

Appreciation is also extended to Dr. Ntuli A. Kapologwe—Director of Health, Social Welfare and Nutrition Services (PO-RALG), for initiating the development of the handbook and facilitating its completion and Mr. Edward Mmbaga—Director of Policy and Planning, Mr. Lusajo Ndagile—Assistant Director of Policy and Planning (MoH). In the same way, appreciation is extended to Dr. Paul Chaote—Assistant Director of Health, Social Welfare and Nutrition Services (PO-RALG), Dr. Yahaya Hussein, Dr. Boniface Richard, Mr. Raymond Kiwesa, Ms. Juliana Mawalla, Ms. Sarah Hussein, Dr. Jumanne Mwasamila and Dr. Bakari Salum for coordination and provision of technical inputs during the whole process of developing this handbook.

The authors acknowledge the financial support provided by Pathfinder International. Acknowledgment is particularly extended to Dr. Joseph Komwihangiro (country director), Dr. Isihaka Mwandalima, Mr. Meshack Mollel and George Binde from Pathfinder International, who worked closely with experts to ensure the successful development of the first draft of this handbook. Indebtedness is protracted to Amref Health Africa Tanzania, USAID Afya Southern Program, HJF Medical Research International, Inc, the Elizabeth Glaser Pediatric AIDS Foundation (EGPAF) and the Centre of Excellence in Health Monitoring and Evaluation of Mzumbe University for providing the financial support to finalize the handbook.

Appreciation is further extended to all stakeholders, specifically the regional and district medical officers, medical officers, health facility in-charges and health secretaries, to mention a few, who provided their input during the stakeholders' meetings.

About the Editors

Mackfallen G. Anasel Dr. Anasel is a senior lecturer and researcher in the Department of Health Systems Management, School of Public Administration and Management at Mzumbe University. He is an accomplished scholar, researcher, teacher, management, administration, governance, leadership specialist, consultant, reproductive and child health specialist, and monitoring and evaluation expert. He has more than 12 years of teaching experience and conducting long and short courses in the areas of health systems management and monitoring, evaluation and learning.

Ntuli A. Kapologwe Dr. Kapologwe has served as District Medical Officer —Bahi and Regional Medical Officer—Shinyanga. Since January 2017, he has served as Director of Health, Social Welfare and Nutrition Services at the President's Office—Regional Administration and Local Government. He has exercised leadership in many institutions, associations, alumni organizations and works on a number of committees at both the national and international levels. He has more than 60 articles published in international peer-reviewed journals.

Albino Kalolo Dr. Kalolo is a senior lecturer and researcher in the Department of Public Health, Faculty of Medicine at St. Francis University College of Health and Allied Sciences, Ifakara, Tanzania. He has a professional background in medicine and public health. His research focuses on implementation science, health system reforms and innovations specifically in primary healthcare, noncommunicable diseases and theory-driven evaluations of health system interventions.

About the Contributors

Anosisye Mwandulusya Kesale Dr. Kesale is a lecturer at Mzumbe University's School of Public Administration and Management. His broad expertise and interests include local governance, leadership health systems strengthening, performance management and health policies. He has eleven years of experience working with national and international organizations in research, consulting and capacity building initiatives.

Boniphace Richard Marwa Dr. Marwa is a principal medical officer currently working in the Simiyu Regional Secretariat as Regional Medical Officer since 2021. He is leading Health Services, Nutrition and Social Welfare in the region with core functions of planning, overseeing, advocating, supervising, monitoring and evaluating performance of the health system. As a District Medical Officer, he was in charge of health services at the district level for nine years (2009–2018).

Godfrey Kacholi Dr. Kacholi has been working at Mzumbe University as an academic staff member in the Department of Health Systems Management since 2011. He is currently the Secretary of the East African Journal of Applied Health Monitoring and Evaluation hosted by Mzumbe University. His primary research interests include quality improvement in the health sector, international health, monitoring and evaluation, hospital management and social welfare system strengthening.

Idda Lyatonga Swai Dr. Swai is a senior lecturer and researcher in the Department of Local Government Management, School of Public Administration and Management at Mzumbe University. She has more than 14 years of experience teaching and conducting long and short courses in the areas of local governance, leadership and gender. She has been coordinating continuous professional development for the Centre for Disease Control project implemented by the centre of excellence in health monitoring and evaluation of Mzumbe University.

James Kengia Dr. Kengia works at the President's Office–Regional Administration and Local Government as a coordinator for regional health management teams, research and publication. He is an experienced public health specialist with a demonstrated history of working in hospitals and the healthcare industry in general. He has also worked as a member of the Regional Referral Hospital Management Team and the Regional Health Management Team and as Regional Medical Officer.

Mwandu Kini Jiyenze Mr. Jiyenze served as a member of the council hospital, council and regional health management teams for five years. Currently, he is a teaching staff member at the Centre for Educational Development in Health Arusha and provides consultancies on health management, planning and policy. He has research interests in health management, health planning and policy.

Leadership and Governance

1

Ntuli A. Kapologwe, Idda Lyatonga Swai, Anosisye Mwandulusya Kesale and James Kengia

Contents

1.1 BACKGROUND INFORMATION

The concepts of leadership and governance are relatively new to health systems (Smith et al., 2012). The definition of leadership focuses on leaders' traits and attributes, exercising of power and influence, roles and relationships between leaders and subordinates. The definition of governance, on the other hand, focuses on a set of values, policies and institutions through which social, economic and political processes are managed on the basis of interaction among the government, civil society and private sectors. Leadership is the ability of a person to influence the behavior of others to willingly take responsibility to accomplish or achieve a common goal. It is about the ability to convince or seek compliance from followers and, by doing so, to comply with the directives

DOI: 10.1201/9781003346821-1

or wishes of the leader to achieve a common purpose. Leadership is defined as a social influence process in which the leader seeks the voluntary participation of subordinates in an effort to reach organizational goals (Afegbua & Adejuwon, 2012). Followers are an important part of the leadership process, and all leaders are sometimes followers as well (Daft, 2014). Leadership is the most influential factor in shaping organizational culture and ensuring direction, alignment and commitment within teams and organizations. In the health system, leadership is the ability of health managers to influence their subordinates to willingly accept their responsibilities and perform them to achieve health system outcomes (Daft, 2014). Therefore, it is expected that health managers will not only use managerial powers and authorities to run health institutions but will also apply leadership skills and techniques to complement managerial power in the course of managing their health institutions.

Governance is about how society, organizations and individual groups make and implement collective choices. It comprises shifting decision-making responsibilities from individuals to a governing authority, with implementation by one or more institutions and with accountability systems to monitor and assure the progress of the decisions taken. Governance in the health system is the way in which powers and control are exercised and shared among health stakeholders over health facilities for the best interest of the whole community. For instance, governance in the health sector involves a variety of stakeholders who share a common set of interests, privileges and means of community control. In order to operate a health system or a health facility, professionals in leadership and managerial positions must coordinate and support the efforts of all stakeholders to provide input for improving the health system.

Strong leadership contributes to good governance by facilitating inter-agency collaboration, common understanding and defined roles and duties. Approaches to leadership and governance, particularly in healthcare systems, vary substantially (Smith et al., 2012). Leadership contributes to good governance by ensuring that the requirements of clients, patients and healthcare providers remain at the forefront of the agenda. Indeed, leaders at all levels give health stakeholders opportunities to offer support in enhancing the effectiveness of the healthcare system. In turn, governance structure provides strategic direction for leaders, helps to build commitment and shared goals and holds individuals accountable.

Governance frameworks play an important role in providing strategic direction for leadership and establishing accountability arrangements, which is partly leadership and partly governance. When things are taken under scrutiny, the process is governance and the way it is pitched is leadership. While leadership sets a direction and makes sure that it happens, governance maintains accountability. Accountability is central to ensuring that decision making is transparent and consequently allows leadership to flourish. Governance, as a structural and important element of monitoring and evaluation, is put in place to underpin the leadership focus on improving health outcomes. Governance directs leadership and provides boundaries for leadership.

The leadership and governance block of the health system is central to improving the performance of the healthcare system and achieving Universal Health Coverage. The World Health Organization (WHO) category of leadership and governance is among the health system building blocks, along with service delivery, health workforce, health information systems, health commodities and technologies and health financing. The leadership and governance building block is viewed as the cornerstone for proper operation of other WHO building blocks. This is due to the fact that the leadership and governance block is a cross-cutting component that provides the basis for the overall policy and regulation of all other health system blocks (Manyazewal, 2017; World Health Organization, 2010). Leadership and governance play a coordinating role at any level of the health system to make sure all other health systems run efficiently and effectively and improve the performance of the health system. Therefore, leadership and governance in the health sector can also be operationalized as new organizational practices and policies, best use of all types of resources, appropriate use of staff working hours, satisfaction of clients and providers and capacity of health facilities to collect, utilize and manage resources (Manyazewal, 2017; Savedoff & Smith, 2011). Through leadership and governance, both health managers and health stakeholders such as communities, civil societies and the private sector define their boundaries, roles and influence in health service provisions.

Different aspects of the health system building blocks require unique leadership and governance mechanisms to be effective (Fryatt et al., 2017). For instance, procurement of health commodities and medical supplies requires governing entities to make decisions on the services to be provided, the roles of the purchaser(s) and providers and the level of resources required to meet service entitlements and improve access (Pezzola & Sweet, 2016). To ensure that health workers perform to the desired standard, leadership and governance are essential. This can be accomplished by health managers when they make critical leadership decisions to enhance the performance of health workers, such as through hiring, training and development, performance management, motivation and disciplinary action. These differences have an influence on the measurement of governance. Governance in the health sector is measured based on its determinants and outcomes (Savedoff, 2011), whether a governing entity is in place and functioning (structure), whether the decisions made are being implemented (process) and whether there is desired improvement in the performance of health outcomes (Greer et al., 2016; Savedoff & Smith, 2011). Governance and leadership are thus critical due to the fact that most conceptualizations and descriptions of health systems developed over the past decade refer to aspects of governance in terms of stewardship, regulation, oversight or governance itself and its effectiveness in the health sector (Fryatt et al., 2017).

In Tanzania, reports from various supportive supervisions and assessments conducted by the MoH and PO-RALG in primary healthcare facilities found that weak leadership and governance practices are among the major hindrances to the delivery of quality health services in Tanzania. For instance, the assessment conducted by PO-RALG in 2020 to evaluate the performance of constructed and renovated health centers that provide comprehensive emergency obstetric and newborn care (CEmONC) services indicated that over 95% of health centers were manned by medical doctors, according to central government directives. However, most of these medical doctors were newly recruited to public services and had never been oriented on leadership and managerial roles or responsibilities. It was also found that there was no guideline that provided practical guidance to these doctors in managing health facilities and related health services. The development of a practical handbook guide for quick reference was deemed important to provide practical guidance to the health facilities in-charge and management teams. This guide aims to promote the practice of good leadership and governance at the primary healthcare level.

This handbook covers and provides practical guidance on the following dimensions of good governance:

(i) **Participation:** All key actors should have a voice in decision making (assessment, planning, management, evaluation) for health, either directly or indirectly. The government in many countries today pledges their citizens to come forward and participate in decision making to debate on complex and difficult issues (Davies et al., 2006; Dent, 2007). Participation is seen as empowerment by handing over a degree of control to improve responsiveness. Participation in healthcare decision making is categorized into three dimensions: (1) information exchange, (2) deliberation and (3) control over the final decision. Patients are the key stakeholders in healthcare whose preferences for each of the dimensions vary and thus reflect the complex nature of their engagement when it comes to participation in healthcare visits (Davies et al., 2006)

(ii) **Transparency:** Transparency is one of the crucial elements of good governance in facilitating decision making and better health outcomes. Existence, sharing and use of result-oriented information and audit-reporting mechanisms are key factors to understand and monitor health matters and resources. Transparency allows both leaders and subordinates to monitor the implementation of activities and evaluation of their performance. Increased transparency in healthcare management, policy and practice can facilitate the important prioritizations that are likely needed over the next decade (Afegbua & Adejuwon, 2012; Jaffe et al., 2006).

(iii) **Accountability**: Leadership and governance approaches highlight issues of state responsiveness and accountability, as well as the impact of these factors on the development of health systems (Afegbua & Adejuwon, 2012). Health managers and staff in health facilities are accountable to the public and to institutional stakeholders. There are theoretical relations between transparency and accountability, such that when transparency exists, accountability is likely to be in place. Transparency facilitates horizontal accountability, strengthens vertical accountability and reduces the need for accountability. Under certain conditions and situations, transparency contributes and facilitates accountability when there is a significant increase in the available information and utilization of the same information, especially when there is a direct or indirect impact on the government or public agency (Meijer, 2014). Strong community health system accountability in primary healthcare is vital to creating accountable community health systems (Kesale et al., 2022; Kessy, 2014).

(iv) **Responsiveness**: Responsiveness in health services refers to meeting the expectations of clients and caregivers. Health managers and health facilities are expected to serve all stakeholders to ensure that the policies, programs and services are responsive to the health and non-health needs of its users. Clients' views and opinions are being recognized as an appropriate measurement of health system responsiveness (Robone et al., 2011). The concept of responsiveness is multi-dimensional and is measured across various domains, including prompt attention, dignity, communication, autonomy, choice of provider, quality of facilities, confidentiality and access to family support (Kapologwe et al., 2020; Mohammed et al., 2013)

(v) **Health equity**: All men and women should have opportunities to improve or maintain their health and well-being, or "the absence of systematic disparities in health (or in the major social determinants of health) between groups with different levels of underlying social advantage/disadvantage—such as wealth, power, or prestige" (Braveman & Gruskin, 2003). Pursuing health equity means striving for the highest possible standard of health for all people and giving special attention to the needs of those at the greatest risk of poor health based on social conditions (Braveman, 2014). Health equity must take into account how resources are allocated and social arrangement is linked with other features of the state of affairs (Sen et al., 2004).

(vi) **Effectiveness and efficiency**: Processes and organizations should produce results that meet population needs, influence health outcomes and make the best use of resources. Common measures of organizational performance are effectiveness and efficiency (Bartuševičienė & Šakalytė, 2013). Health organizations assess their performance in terms of effectiveness, focusing on the extent to which they have achieved their mission, goals, vision and efficiency in terms of the resources used to achieve the goals.

(vii) **Rule of law**: Refers to the presence and impartial enforcement of policies, laws, regulations and guidelines pertaining to health. The Rule of Law, accountability and transparency are technical and legal issues that interact to produce institutions that are legitimate and effective by ensuring the enforcement of policies, laws and regulations (Johnston, 2006). Legitimate institutions are entrusted by the people and provide law and order, protect fundamental human rights and ensure rule of law and due process of law (Afegbua & Adejuwon, 2012).

(viii) **Ethics:** Ethics is concerned with the rules and standards for determining what is "correct" conduct and behavior. The idea that ethics is important in any organization is central to healthcare systems (Kolthoff, 2007). Ethics is about following or adhering to accepted principles of healthcare ethics in health service provision and research, or promoting ethical management and standards among health professionals. Ethics determine how the organizational objective/goals are established and implemented, as well as the ethical reasoning that involves explaining how the decisions were reached. Healthcare organizations are likely to face new, business-oriented ethical issues due to changes in the delivery and financing of healthcare. Addressing these issues, among others, requires clear guidance of healthcare professionals to ensure that healthcare ethical standards are ensured in the whole process of delivery of primary healthcare.

1.2 ORGANIZATION OF THE HEALTHCARE SYSTEMS IN TANZANIA

The national healthcare system operates under a decentralized system of governance. It is organized in a referral pyramid, made up of three main levels: (1) primary level, (2) secondary level and (3) tertiary level. This guide is intended for the primary level.

At the primary level, council and all other hospitals are referral centers for all primary health facilities, including both public and private dispensaries and health centers. The facilities at this level are fully fledged to provide services to both inpatient and outpatient clients. In the current arrangement, the local government authorities through their technical team—for example, a council health management team (CHMT) headed by a district medical officer (DMO)—have a full mandate for planning, implementation, monitoring and evaluation of health services within the council.

1.3 WHAT IS THE PURPOSE OF THIS PRACTICAL HANDBOOK?

The purpose of this practical handbook is to provide guidance on leadership and governance issues in primary healthcare facilities and to improve the quality of health service provisions. Furthermore, the guide is envisaged to serve as a quick, day-to-day reference for leading and managing all facility operations. The facility operations in this guide revolve around six WHO health system building blocks, where leadership and governance are unpacked as they play out in each of the other building blocks.

1.4 FOR WHOM WAS THIS PRACTICAL HANDBOOK DESIGNED?

The handbook is for everyone involved in the management of health facilities at the primary health facility level. More specifically, the guide is designed for health facility in-charges, health facility management teams (HFMTs), facility quality improvement teams (FQITs), heads of sections/units, facility medicine and therapeutic committees (FMTCs) and working improvement teams (WITs).

1.5 HOW WAS THIS PRACTICAL HANDBOOK DEVELOPED?

In October 2020, the MoH and PO-RALG convened in a panel of individuals from different institutions with expertise in healthcare service delivery, health systems, local government, leadership and governance and shared reports highlighting weak leadership and governance that affected the delivery of quality services in primary healthcare in Tanzania. The reports further indicated that most of the health centers were manned by medical doctors who were newly recruited and had never been oriented to leadership and managerial roles. The panel came to a consensus to develop a practical handbook and implementation plans informed by the best available evidence to serve as a guide. The process of developing this handbook involved the following steps:

(i) **Inception meeting:** An inception meeting between experts and management of the PO-RALG and MoH was held to share and digest various assessments and supportive supervision reports conducted in the primary healthcare facilities. Weak leadership and governance in the primary healthcare facilities was among the major concerns that needed immediate attention. This called for the development of a practical guide handbook to serve as a quick reference for managers of health facilities. Experts were given terms of reference to guide the development of the practical handbook.

(ii) **Desk review:** Experts in collaboration with the technical team from the PO-RALG conducted a desk review. The review was aimed at identifying leadership and governance elements that were not featured in the assessments, along with supportive supervision reports. Through desk review, the components of governance that were either left out or omitted in the assessments and supportive supervision reports were captured and embedded in WHO's six health building blocks to inform the development of the practical handbook to suit the Tanzanian context.

(iii) **Development of a draft practical handbook:** The development of the draft practical handbook was guided by the information gathered from the inception meeting and the desk review.

(iv) **Stakeholder's forum:** The draft of a practical handbook that was developed based on the assessment and desk review was presented to stakeholders. The stakeholders included representatives from dispensaries and health centers, medical officers in charge (MOIs), district medical officers (DMOs), regional medical officers (RMOs), district health secretaries (DHSs), regional health secretaries (RHSs) and officials from both the MoH and the PO-RALG. The stakeholders provided technical and practical experiences in managing health facilities. Their inputs contributed significantly to improving the contents and the structure of the draft. Specifically, the stakeholders developed two scenarios that have been included in this practical guide.

(v) **Ministerial review workshop:** The draft practical guide was presented to the management and staff of the PO-RALG and MoH, as well as co-opted members from the regional health management team (RHMT), council health management team (CHMT) and facility health management team (FHMT), and their input facilitated improvement and finalization of the guide. The ministry officials provided policy implementation practices and experiences regarding the management of health facilities that were very pertinent in shaping the finalization of the practical guide.

1.6 REFERENCES

Afegbua, S. I., & Adejuwon, K. D. (2012). The challenges of leadership and governance in Africa. *International Journal of Academic Research in Business and Social Sciences, 2*(9), 141.

Bartuševičienė, I., & Šakalytė, E. (2013). Organizational assessment: Effectiveness vs. efficiency. *Social Transformations in Contemporary Society, 1*(1), 45–53.

Braveman, P. (2014). What are health disparities and health equity? We need to be clear. *Public Health Reports, 129*(Suppl 2), 5–8.

Braveman, P., & Gruskin, S. (2003). Defining equity in health. *Journal of Epidemiology & Community Health, 57*, 254–258. https://jech.bmj.com/content/57/4/254

Daft, R. L. (2014). *The leadership experience*. Cengage Learning.

Davies, C., Wetherell, M., & Barnett, E. (2006). *Citizens at the centre: Deliberative participation in healthcare decisions*. Policy Press.

Dent, M. (2007). Citizens at the centre: Deliberative participation in healthcare decisions—by Davies, C., Wetherell, M., & E. Barnett. *Sociology of Health & Illness, 29*(5), 787–788. https://doi.org/10.1111/j.1467-9566.2007.01039_1.x

Fryatt, R., Bennett, S., & Soucat, A. (2017). Health sector governance: Should we be investing more? *BMJ Global Health, 2*(2), e000343. https://doi.org/10.1136/bmjgh-2017-000343

Greer, S., Wismar, M., & Figueras, J. (2016). Introduction: Strengthening governance amidst changing governance. In *Strengthening health system governance: Better policies, stronger performance* (pp. 3–26). McGraw-Hill.

Jaffe, R., Nash, R. A., Ash, R., Schwartz, N., Corish, R., Born, T., & Lazarus, H. (2006). Healthcare transparency: Opportunity or mirage. *Journal of Management Development, 25*(10), 981–995.

Johnston, M. (2006). *Good governance: Rule of law, transparency, and accountability* (pp. 1–32). United Nations Public Administration Network.

Kapologwe, N. A., Kibusi, S. M., Borghi, J., Gwajima, D. O., & Kalolo, A. (2020). Assessing health system responsiveness in primary health care facilities in Tanzania. *BMC Health Services Research, 20*(1), 104.

Kesale, A. M., Mahonge, C., & Muhanga, M. (2022). The quest for accountability of health facility governing committees implementing direct health facility financing in Tanzania: A supply-side experience. *Plos One, 17*(4), e0267708.

Kessy, F. L. (2014). Improving health services through empowered community health governance structures in Tanzania. *Journal of Rural and Community Development, 9*(2), Article 2. https://journals.brandonu.ca/jrcd/article/view/826

Kolthoff, E. W. (2007). *Ethics and new public management: Empirical research into the effects of businesslike government on ethics and integrity.* https://research.vu.nl/en/publications/ethics-and-new-public-management-empirical-research-into-the-effe

Manyazewal, T. (2017). Using the world health organization health system building blocks through survey of healthcare professionals to determine the performance of public healthcare facilities. *Archives of Public Health = Archives Belges De Sante Publique, 75*, 50. https://doi.org/10.1186/s13690-017-0221-9

Meijer, A. (2014). Transparency. In M. Bovens, R. Goodin, & T. Schillemans (Eds.), *The Oxford handbook of public accountability* (online edn., August 4). Oxford Academic. Retrieved November 30, 2022, from https://doi.org/10.1093/oxfordhb/9780199641253.013.0043

Mohammed, S., Bermejo, J. L., Souares, A., Sauerborn, R., & Dong, H. (2013). Assessing responsiveness of health care services within a health insurance scheme in Nigeria: Users' perspectives. *BMC Health Services Research, 13*(1), 1–13.

Pezzola, A., & Sweet, C. M. (2016). Global pharmaceutical regulation: The challenge of integration for developing states. *Globalization and Health, 12*(1), 85. https://doi.org/10.1186/s12992-016-0208-2

Robone, S., Rice, N., & Smith, P. C. (2011). Health systems' responsiveness and its characteristics: A cross-country comparative analysis. *Health Services Research, 46*(6pt2), 2079–2100.

Savedoff, W. D. (2011). *Governance in the health sector: A strategy for measuring determinants and performance.* World Bank Policy Research Working Paper, 5655. World Bank.

Savedoff, W. D., & Smith, A. L. (2011). *Achieving universal health coverage: Learning from Chile, Japan, Malaysia and Sweden.* Results for Development Institute.

Sen, A., Anand, S., & Peter, F. (2004). *Why health equity?* (pp. 21–33). Oxford University Press.

Smith, P. C., Anell, A., Busse, R., Crivelli, L., Healy, J., Lindahl, A. K., Westert, G., & Kene, T. (2012). Leadership and governance in seven developed health systems. *Health Policy, 106*(1), 37–49.

World Health Organization (2010). *Monitoring the building blocks of health systems: A handbook of indicators and their measurement strategies.* World Health Organization. https://apps.who.int/iris/handle/10665/258734

Management and Governance of Health Facilities

2

Anosisye Mwandulusya Kesale and Idda Lyatonga Swai

Contents

2.1 INTRODUCTION

Health system management and governance are cornerstones of health system performance. Indeed, facility management and governance guarantee a smooth running of health facility operations at the primary healthcare level. Embracing good management and governance practices in primary health facilities contributes to the achievement of health facility goals (Desta et al., 2020; Yuan et al., 2017) and the improvement of health outcomes of the population in the catchment area and beyond. Poor performing facilities, on the other hand, are

DOI: 10.1201/9781003346821-2

constrained by their own weaknesses, such as poor management and leadership capacities of the council health management team (CHMT) and lack of motivation among facility staff and allied health workers (Mpambije, 2017). Managing and governing healthcare facilities while encouraging openness, responsibility, participation and responsiveness is a step toward delivering high-quality medical services. Managing and governing health facilities contains two principles that are crucial for the performance of health facilities and the delivery of health services that are responsive, effective and efficient. The first component is the management of health facilities. This entails the general execution of managerial functions at the health facility. Facility management has been a necessary component of high-quality primary healthcare to optimize the effectiveness and efficiency of many health service fields (Desta et al., 2020). The functions include the preparation of facility plans and budgets, supervision of health workers, management of health facility infrastructures, insurance of quality improvement, management of facility finances, procurement and insurance of the availability of health commodities and availability of a functional health information system to ensure health service delivery. The managerial functions should be carried out jointly by the health facility management team under the supervision of the health facility in-charge.

Governance of health facilities is a second component that entails the extent to which a wider range of stakeholders within and surrounding the health facilities jointly participate in decision making on health service provision at the given health facility. This component should be implemented within the facility by exercising governance principles such as participation, transparency, rule of law, accountability and responsiveness. Therefore, facility managers and whoever holds a position in the health facility are expected to engage fellow health workers, be transparent enough, embrace the rule of law, be fair and respond timely to health workers' concerns. Outside of the organization, the health facility management led by the health facility in-charge is expected to engage all health stakeholders such as communities, civil societies, non-governmental organizations, faith-based institutions and the private sector in planning, implementation and evaluation of facility service delivery to increase the functionality of community governance systems (Kesale et al., 2022).

Managing and governing a health facility is an important endeavor that is key to realizing gains in other health system building blocks. Health facility managers have the great role of managing the day-to-day routines of the health facility, including planning for the future of their health facilities. These managers have to play the coordination and integration roles of the health workforce and other resources. The decisions of the health facility in-charge should be collective to create ownership among healthcare workers and a common understanding with other primary healthcare actors. Management and governance are among managerial attributes that enhance linkage and collaborations between the facilities, communities, stakeholders and government structures such as ward development committees (WDCs) and village governments.

In the Tanzanian context, the management of primary health facilities is structured and organized at different levels, starting from the district council to the community. Each level has separate mandates to perform to ensure accountability and checks and balances between the levels. The levels are fundamental for achieving universal health coverage if all work as intended. To effectively carry out their mandates, there are separate management levels and community governance structures. Managerial structures are technical teams composed of technical persons from different areas of specialization within the health system at a particular level. On the other hand, community structures are the structures composed of members of the community who are primarily mandated with oversight roles of the given level of the health system, from the council to the health delivery point. These managerial and community governance structures are explained in detail herewith.

(i) **Management and governance structures of health services:** The healthcare system under local government authority is managed and governed by various structures (organs), which are placed at different levels. At the council level, there is a council health management team (CHMT), while at the lower level of primary healthcare facilities (health centers and dispensaries), there is a health facility management team (HFMT). Each structure has mandates, roles and functions, as elaborated in the subsequent sections.

(ii) **CHMT:** Under the local government authorities, the CHMT is composed of coordinators of specific services within the council health system. The CHMT is led by the council (district) medical officer of a given council. The CHMT is responsible for the coordination of planning, implementation and management of health and welfare services in the council. The CHMT is also responsible for providing technical assistance to the primary healthcare facilities while ensuring direction, alignment and commitment within teams and organizations and making sure that achievements are consistent with the vision, values and strategy of the organization (Desta et al., 2020; Kapologwe et al., 2019). Specifically, the CHMT is responsible for the following:

- Building capacities of the health facilities through coaching and mentorship.
- Performing analysis for continuous management improvement.
- Gathering community opinions regarding priorities and challenges in accessing healthcare services to inform the planning process.

- Preparing council comprehensive health plans (CCHPs) according to the existing national policies and guidelines.
- Supporting health facility teams in developing health facility plans.
- Ensuring that health services are provided as per comprehensive health plans.
- Carrying out supportive supervision of health staff at all levels of the council.
- Collecting, analyzing and utilizing data and providing feedback mechanisms at all levels.
- Monitoring and evaluating the implementation of health activities by the council.
- Collaborating with stakeholders working in the council to ensure that all activities are incorporated into CCHPs.
- Maintaining and liaising with regional health management teams (RHMTs) during the preparation of CCHPs.
- Supporting and ensuring functionality of the council health service board (CHSB) and facility health governing committees (HFGCs).
- Collaborating with and supervising private health facilities within the council.

(iii) **HFMT:** At the primary health facility level, the HFMT is composed of the heads of units and sections of a given health facility. The number of members in that HFMT is determined by the type of the health facility. The HFMT is led by the health facility in-charge. Overall, the HFMT is responsible for planning, coordinating and managing provision of health and social welfare services at the health facility and community levels.

The specific functions of the HFMT are as follows:

- Preparing and executing the facility annual plans and budget.
- Managing income and expenditure of the facility through compliance with the financial guidelines and standards through the facility financial accounting and reporting system (FFARS).
- Monitoring and reviewing facility financial and physical implementation progress of health expenditure against budgets.
- Organizing and mobilizing the community to join the improved community health fund (iCHF) and other health insurances.
- Constructing, renovating and maintaining facility infrastructures and equipment in a timely manner.
- Ensuring that facility organization structure is displayed and known to the staff.
- Assessing performance of health workers.

- Conducting monthly meetings with their subordinates.
- Disseminating and ensuring implementation of policies, rules, regulations, guidelines, standards and government directives.
- Assessing the constraint of facility performance in health service delivery and developing the appropriate solutions.
- Managing the procurement of health commodities according to established policies, regulations and standards.
- Keeping facility records by following regulations and standards.
- Conducting surveillance and rapid response to diseases outbreaks.
- Monitoring the quality of services provided to clients, including patient complaints and satisfaction in the facility.
- Supporting and facilitating functions of health facility governing committees.
- Engaging the community in planning, management, monitoring and evaluation of health services.
- Ensuring that facility quality improvement teams (FQITs), facility medicine and therapeutic committees (FMTCs) and working improvement teams (WITs) are functional.
- Collecting and using facility data for planning and service improvement.

(iv) **Community governance structures:** At the primary healthcare level in Tanzania, community participation is effectively represented through the two established community health governing structures. At the council level, there is a council health service board (CHSB), while at the primary healthcare facilities, there are health facility governing committees. These structures are established to strengthen community participation in the management and governance of health service delivery, as stipulated in health policy and guidelines.

(v) **CHSB:** The CHSB has the following roles and responsibilities:
- Ensuring that the population receives appropriate, quality, affordable and timely healthcare services.
- Discussing and approving health plans, budgets and reports from the CHMT and submitting such reports to the full council for approval.
- Supporting the CHMT in managing and administering health resources.
- Promoting community involvement through sensitization.
- Ensuring distribution and efficient use of resources based on the needs of all levels of service.
- Receiving and analyzing implementation reports from CHMTs.
- Designing various sources of revenue and mobilizing sufficient resources to run council health services.

- Coordinating and supervising health development interventions, including the primary health services development plan (PHSDP; popularly known as "MMAM" in the area of jurisdiction (Council area).
- Advising the council on the availability of staff in accordance with the staffing levels of the council.
- Conducting healthcare monitoring and evaluation activities.

(vi) **Health facility governing committee:** The empowered health facility governing committees are able to oversee healthcare provider accountability and improve health service provision (Kesale et al., 2022). Specifically, the health facility governing committee has the following functions:

- Ensuring that residents have access to affordable health services.
- Ensuring availability of sufficient resources to improve health facility services.
- Receiving, analyzing, reviewing and approving health facility plans prepared by HFMT.
- Receiving and discussing quarterly and annual implementation reports prepared by the HFMT.
- Designing/establishing various sources of revenue and mobilizing sufficient resources to run health facility services.
- Collaborating with other health committees and various stakeholders in the provision and improvement of health services.
- Reporting to the CHSB the staffing gap in accordance with the staffing levels of the relevant facility.
- Involving the community in planning and informing them on the implementation progress of healthcare plans in the health facility.

Figure 2.1 shows the health sector governance structure at the local government authorities (LGAs) in mainland Tanzania. Solid lines indicate administrative interactions, dashed lines indicate technical and political advisory interactions and stakeholders within the dotted box belong to the dispensary and health center. The dispensary and health center are overlapping with the ward and village levels because the health centers and dispensaries are administered at ward and village levels, respectively. The health facility in-charge and the health management team report the facility's performances and challenges to the CHMT. In addition, the facility in-charge is required to attend meetings at ward and village levels to report the facility operations, achievements and challenges. The facility in-charge should collaborate with the village social service committee, which includes multi-sectoral AIDS committees, and other committees dealing with special groups such as the elderly, people with disabilities and children.

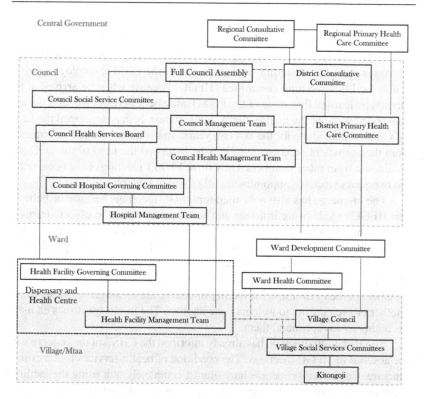

FIGURE 2.1 Health Governance Structure in Local Government Authority

The primary focus of this chapter is to build an understanding of the leadership and management of health facilities by focusing on the key components of leadership and governance, which include transparency, accountability, participation and responsiveness, and linking with the health services and health facility management of the health facility whilst simultaneously improving health outcomes.

2.2 SCENARIO

Isabula Health Centre has been in operation since 2016, but service delivery has been inadequate and unresponsive since then. To address this issue, the district medical officer (DMO) replaced the health facility in-charge in 2018 with a newly recruited medical doctor who graduated in 2017 with the idea that this young and dynamic doctor would improve the facility's operations.

In the course of managing the facility, the in-charge has made all facility decisions without consulting or engaging with the FHMT, employees or the health facility governing committee (HFGC) because when he arrived at the facility, he learned that some of the FHMT members were not trustworthy and embezzled some of the facility funds. For instance, he has developed the facility's annual plan alone for the last two years, and when he needed information from the outpatient department (OPD), he bypassed the head of the OPD and obtained it from other members. Only three FHMT meetings have occurred in the two years since his appointment, all of which took place in 2018.

The in-charge has also not called for HFGC meetings because he believes that HFGC members are illiterate and hence have nothing to offer in terms of professional matters such as health. When the committee chairperson asked the in-charge when the meeting would be held, the in-charge responded that the facility was running low on cash, thus, there was no money to pay the allowance of the HFGC members. As a result of this alarming condition, the members of the FHMT and the facility in-charge are no longer speaking to one another or even daring to welcome one another. The in-charge insists on using his authority to reprimand them.

The HFGC chairperson has already informed the CHSB of the concern with the absence of HFGC meetings. The condition of health services is at a critical juncture. Community residents have almost completely quit using the facility's services in favor of the nearby private hospital. Even individuals who have joined the iCHF are not accessing the facility's services because they do not appreciate its value to the community members from several villages in the ward.

The facility in-charge has never appeared at any of the meetings held by the village government to report on the status of the health facility service provision, using the justification that he had to travel to the district council headquarters to follow up on crucial issues pertaining to the facilities. Even worse, when members of the HFGC were asked by the village government to provide an update on the facility operations, the response was that they were unaware of anything because they had not been informed.

In an open letter to the CHMT, the village government, HFGC and WDC expressed their disappointment with the facility's deficiencies and the health facility manager's inappropriate behavior. The CHMT made the decision to supervise the facility. When they arrived and evaluated the facility's operation, the CHMT was shocked to find the serious issues at the facility and realized that the WDC, HFGC and village government's complaints were very much genuine. The CHMT made the decision to suspend the in-charge of the health facility and asked the Prevention and Combating of Corruption Bureau (PCCB) to investigate the conduct of the in-charge and any abuse of power and authority.

2.2.1 Consider these Questions

1. What are the key leadership and governance challenges experienced by this facility?
2. Does your health facility experience similar challenges?
3. What could be the possible causes of these problems?
4. Can these challenges be resolved by a person or by the collective efforts of the health system?

2.2.2 Reflection

This situation serves as a reminder of the value of knowledge and abilities in leadership and governance for the management of healthcare facilities. Health facility management is supposed to be a collaborative effort, not the sole responsibility of one person. The in-charge prepared the facility plans, made all decisions pertaining to the facility and neither organized nor attended any meetings at the facility, village or ward level. These decisions were made without consulting any authorities, structures or bodies at the facility, ward or council level. The facility in-charge displayed poor knowledge and abilities of governance and leadership and, as a result, was penalized. This scenario also informs managers of the importance of abiding to management principles and incorporating this practical handbook package in newly recruited staff induction courses/training.

2.2.3 Addressing the Problem and Developing an Action Plan

Step 1: Addressing the Problem

The aforementioned managerial challenges could be addressed by doing the following:

(i) **Participation**
- Involving the FHMT and HFGC in the preparation of the facility's annual plan and budget.
- Having the HFGC read, discuss and endorse the annual plan and budget.
- Conducting monthly FHMT meetings to discuss the operation of the facility.
- Presenting facility operations in the HFGC meetings.
- Engaging relevant authorities in the facility, village, ward and council to solve facility challenges.

(ii) **Transparency**
- Sharing all information from the upper level (council level) with the HFMT, health workers and HFGC in line with the guidelines.
- Discussing facility annual plans and budget activities with each member of the facility management team and their subordinates.
- Discussing income and expenditure of the facility with staff and publishing it on the facility notice board.
- Presenting operations of the facility to the HFGC at quarterly meetings.
- Presenting the status of service provision, facility plans and activities to the WDC and at village meetings.

(iii) **Accountability**
- Conducting monthly health facility management meetings.
- Submitting financial information to the HFGC and CHMT.
- Aligning facility activities with the annual plan and budget.
- Disclosing the client service charter to the health workers, clients and community.
- Conducting department/section meetings before the FHMT meeting.
- Attending WDC and village/Mtaa meetings.
- Conducting a monthly client satisfaction exit survey.
- Publishing and informing the community on the costs of health services, delivery options and available resources.

(iv) **Responsiveness**
- Supervising the implementation of FHMT meeting resolutions.
- Preparing and using a plan of action to address community challenges and provide feedback.
- Addressing clients' and patients' issues and challenges and providing feedback through available mechanisms.
- Motivating staff by rewarding best performers, punishing poor performers and proactively addressing aggressive, inappropriate and unacceptable behaviors displayed by staff in accordance with governing rules and regulations.

(v) **Linkages and collaborations**
- The link between facility management teams and CHMTs:
  - The FHMT should submit to the CHMT quarterly and annual financial reports and reports on the implementation of the facility plan.
  - Requests to use funds should be submitted to the DMO in a timely manner.

- The link between the FHMT, the WDC and village assemblies:
  - The facility in-charge should have regular meetings and discussions with community resource persons, such as community health workers and volunteers.
  - The facility in-charge has to submit a progress implementation report at WDC and village meetings.
  - The health in-charge has to attend all WDC and village/Mtaa meetings.
  - The health in-charge has to participate in all development activities and campaigns conducted by the WDC and village assembly.
  - The FHMT has to collect views and health challenges from the WDC and village meetings and address them.
  - The report on the status of the iCHF should be submitted to the Ward Health Committee.
- The link between the facility and other stakeholders:
  - Establish a relationship with both private and non-government organizations to tape resources for improving service provision.

Step 2: Developing an Action Plan

After problem analysis, the facility in-charge is required to develop an action plan that will address the identified shortfalls using the correct measure(s). This action plan should be used to undertake self-assessment and catalyze analysis of the identified problems. In order to develop the action plan, the facility in-charge should state and describe the problem, identify potential causes of the problems, propose strategies to address the problems, suggest the responsible person to address the problem and follow timelines, as indicated by the example in Table 2.1.

2.2.4 Other Potential Issues

The proposed solutions based on the aforementioned scenario aim to give an overview of how the leadership of the facility can address day-to-day challenges affecting the functioning of the health facilities. It is important to note that the issues presented in the scenario are not exhaustive. This chapter suggests that the health facility in-charge and other FHMT members should always consider other potential issues while executing their functions. Examples of other potential issues are presented in Box 2.1.

TABLE 2.1 An Action Plan for Managing a Health Facility

PROBLEM	DESCRIPTION OF THE PROBLEM	POTENTIAL CAUSES OF THE PROBLEM	PROPOSED ACTIVITIES TO ADDRESS THE PROBLEM	RESPONSIBLE PERSON	DEADLINE FOR ADDRESSING THE PROBLEM
Weak Teamwork	The health facility in-charge was performing the facility activities alone without engaging other members, including the FHMT.	• No orientation or coaching • Lack of skills to build and work with teams	• Conduct orientation and coaching to newly appointed managers • Take initiative to learn from other experienced managers • Prepare a meeting schedule that will govern the FHMT meetings • Provide on-job training on building and working with a team	Facility in-charge	Two weeks after developing an action plan
Lack of meetings	HFGC and FHMT meetings were not conducted on a quarterly and monthly basis	• No time tables • No supervision or coaching • Failure to follow guidelines	• Conduct supervision and coaching • Prepare a timetable • Conduct monthly meetings • Keep FHMT Meetings records • Go through guidelines	Facility in-charge	Within a week of the development of an action plan

Issue	Finding		Action	Responsible	Timeline
Poor relationship between the facility, community and other government structures/stakeholders	There have been claims that the facility in-charge was not sharing or involving the HFGC, village government or other stakeholders in the facility actions	• No orientation • Not attending village meetings • Not organizing HFGC meetings	• Conduct supportive supervision and orientation • Organize HFGC meetings quarterly • Attend WDC and village meetings	Facility in-charge	Within a week of the development of an action plan
	Healthcare workers were not seen to be engaged with local community concerns related to healthcare delivery	• No awareness • No plan	• Conduct coaching • Prepare a plan • Engage in local community concerns related to healthcare delivery	Facility in-charge	Immediately
	The Facility Health Management Team did not plan specific interventions to address local health concerns and improve services	• No timetable for FHMT meetings • Poor relationship between the in-charge and FHMT	• Perform orientation/coaching • Plan for specific interventions to address local health concerns and improve services	Facility in-charge	Immediately
	HFGC did not give feedback to the broader community	• No HFGC meetings	• Conduct HFGC meetings • Give feedback to the village/ward social service committee or village/ward assembly	Facility in-charge	Two weeks after development of an action plan

BOX 2.1   POTENTIALS ISSUES TO BE CONSIDERED

1. Compliance with government directives.
2. Preparation for disaster and epidemic management.
3. Awareness of available disciplinary structures, professional boards and professional councils.
4. Understanding of community and other stakeholder expectations.
5. Familiarity with all guidelines, rules, public service standing orders, policies and codes of conduct that govern health service provisions.

2.3 REFERENCES

Desta, B. F., Abitew, A., Beshir, I. A., Argaw, M. D., & Abdlkader, S. (2020). Leadership, governance and management for improving district capacity and performance: The case of USAID transform: Primary health care. *BMC Family Practice, 21*(1), 252. https://doi.org/10.1186/s12875-020-01337-0

Kapologwe, N. A., Kalolo, A., Kibusi, S. M., Chaula, Z., Nswilla, A., Teuscher, T., Aung, K., & Borghi, J. (2019). Understanding the implementation of direct health facility financing and its effect on health system performance in Tanzania: A non-controlled before and after mixed method study protocol. *Health Research Policy and Systems, 17*(1), 11. https://doi.org/10.1186/s12961-018-0400-3

Kesale, A. M., Mahonge, C., & Muhanga, M. (2022). The functionality variation among health facility governing committees under direct health facility financing in Tanzania. *PLOS Global Public Health, 2*(5), e0000366. https://doi.org/10.1371/journal.pgph.0000366

Mpambije, C. J. (2017). Decentralisation of health systems and the fate of community health fund in Tanzania: Critical review of high and low performing districts. *Science Journal of Public Health, 5*(2), 136. https://doi.org/10.11648/j.sjph.20170502.21

Yuan, B., Jian, W., He, L., Wang, B., & Balabanova, D. (2017). The role of health system governance in strengthening the rural health insurance system in China. *International Journal for Equity in Health, 16*(1), 44. https://doi.org/10.1186/s12939-017-0542-x

Health Service Delivery

3

Albino Kalolo and Mwandu Kini Jiyenze

Contents

3.1 INTRODUCTION

Leadership and governance are driving forces toward the provision of quality health services. Good governance and leadership in the healthcare system are prerequisites for optimal operation of health service delivery building block (Smith et al., 2012; World Health Organization, 2010). Service provision, as an immediate output of the health system inputs such as health workforce, procurement and supplies and financing, is expected to ensure the availability

DOI: 10.1201/9781003346821-3

of health services that meet a minimum quality standard (Manzi et al., 2012; World Health Organization, 2007; Yip et al., 2015). In any well-functioning health system, service delivery should have the following key characteristics (World Health Organization, 2010):

(i) **Comprehensiveness:** A broad range of health services appropriate to the needs of the target population is delivered, including preventative, curative, palliative and rehabilitative services and health promotion activities.

(ii) **Accessibility:** Services are directly and permanently accessible with no undue barriers of cost, language, culture, gender, physicality or geography. Services may be provided in the health facilities, the community (through outreach and mobile services), the workplace or the home, as appropriate.

(iii) **Coverage:** Service delivery is designed so that all people in a defined target population are covered, that is, the sick and the healthy, all income groups and all social groups.

(iv) **Continuity:** Service delivery is organized to provide an individual with continuity of care across the network of services, health conditions and levels of care, and over their life cycle.

(v) **Quality:** Health services are of high quality, that is, they are effective, safe, centered on the patient's needs and given in a timely fashion.

(vi) **Person-centeredness:** Services are organized around the person, not the disease or the financing. Users perceive health services to be responsive and acceptable for them. There is participation from the target population in service delivery design and assessment. People are partners in their own healthcare. The person is not only the client/patient but the family, relative and caretakers are also included.

(vii) **Coordination:** Local area health service networks are actively coordinated across types of providers, types of care, levels of service delivery and for both routine and emergency preparedness. The primary healthcare provider works in collaboration with other levels and providers to facilitate a smooth route through which the patient and client receives needed services. Coordination also takes place with other sectors (e.g. social services) and partners (e.g. community organizations).

(viii) **Accountability and efficiency:** Health services are well managed so as to achieve the aforementioned core elements with minimum wastage of resources. Managers are allocated the necessary authority to achieve planned objectives and are held accountable for overall performance and results. Assessment includes appropriate mechanisms for the participation of the target population and civil society.

In order to manage the health service, there is a need for service delivery monitoring. Shortage of medicines, uneven distribution of both health service and human resource workforces, including poor availability of equipment or guidelines, must all be taken into account as parts of basic service management. This could be possible if leadership and governance issues are taken into account in the health service delivery building block.

This chapter on health service delivery intends to give a highlight of the role of leadership and governance, focusing on the facility-based and community health services in the catchment area. The key elements of leadership and governance to be addressed by this chapter include equity, transparency, accountability, professionalism and ethics, participation, responsiveness and quality of services.

3.2 SCENARIO ONE

Sikitu, a 39-year-old widow living with her four children in a village located 30 km from the district hospital, presented with symptoms of cervical cancer when she went to see a doctor at a public district hospital. She had been coming to the hospital almost every month for the past year or so to see a certain doctor. She had always paid the doctor after the services, but the problem was still going on despite the fact that some procedures (*"kusafishwa"*) had been performed on her. She was then scheduled to come again regularly for follow-up visits and was required to pay some money whenever she accessed services.

Upon one of her follow up visits, she happened to be attended by another doctor who was on duty. After a physical examination, Sikitu asked the doctor, *"how much should I pay you for all these services I have received?"* The doctor replied, cancer services in this country are offered for free (without payment), like other services which are also exempted by policy such as HIV/AIDS, services for under-five children and pregnant women; you are also not supposed to pay directly to the doctor if there are associated costs.

Sikitu was surprised to hear that and was pretty much speechless when she reflected on what had been happening to her and other poor people. Then she burst into tears. When asked why she was crying, she explained that she was very surprised that all this time, she had been suffering from a disease that she wasn't told about, and she was paying for free services. The doctor later referred her to the cancer institute in Dar es Salaam for further treatment on account of advanced cervical cancer. She went home and sold the few goats she had to get money for her travel and living expenses (for when she receives treatment in Dar es Salaam).

3.2.1 Consider these Questions

1. How many people experience a similar situation to the scenario described here?
2. What might be the cause of the governance challenges experienced in this scenario?
3. What are the roles of the in-charge of the health facility and the management team to address the governance challenges experienced in this scenario?
4. What could be looked at during internal supportive supervision at the health facility to address governance challenges?

3.2.2 Reflection

This scenario reminds the in-charge of the health facility and HMT of the barriers to accessing quality healthcare, especially among the poor segment of the population, which is the majority in our communities. Most of the barriers to quality care experienced at the facility level are results of poor leadership and governance of health service delivery. Sikitu was forced to pay for services that are exempted by policy and also received inappropriate care for the problem she was having.

This points out the problems of accountability and professional misconduct among health workers in the facility where she was receiving care. Moreover, it is clear that there was a lack of transparency at the health facility in terms of displaying to clients the services offered at the health facility and associated costs. Sikitu should have known if the services required payments and where to pay, instead of paying directly to the doctor.

3.2.3 Addressing the Problem and Developing an Action Plan

Step 1: Addressing the Problem

The governance and leadership issues in health service delivery presented in this scenario relate to transparency, accountability, equity and quality of health services. To address these aspects of governance and leadership, the in-charges should:

(i) **Transparency**
- publicly display all health services provided at the facility and their costs (elaborate on which ones are offered for free and which ones are paid out of pocket or through health insurance).
- provide daily announcements during health education regarding the health services provided, their costs and a list of the exempted services for those who cannot read.
- inform the council health service board (CHSB), the ward development committee (WDC) or the village council and the community health workers (CHWs) of the health services provided, including their costs and all other exempted services.

(ii) **Accountability**
- follow up on clinical and nursing care of patients by obtaining reports from the outpatient and inpatient service points on a daily basis and comparing them with the revenue collected.
- conduct internal supportive supervision in all departments and sections in the health facility.
- take disciplinary action against staff who do not abide by professional standards and ethics through appropriate disciplinary structures and professional bodies.

(iii) **Equity**
- provide all services to all groups, paying attention to vulnerable groups such as children, pregnant women, indigents and the elderly.
- provide patient-centered services regardless of any vulnerability, such as social exclusion or socioeconomic status.

(iv) **Quality of health services**

- ensure that quality improvement teams (QITs) meet regularly (as per guidelines) to discuss and deliberate on quality improvement issues.
- ensure that QITs regularly provide quality assessment of the health services provided.
- abide by all guidelines, standard operating procedures (SOPs) and protocols in service provision sites (departments, units, wards) and review their utilization.
- conduct data quality assessments (DQAs) and data review meetings (DRMs) monthly. The data synthesized from the health management information system (HIMS), resolutions from meetings and research should be used to improve the quality of services conducted weekly during continuous professional development (CPD) sessions at the health facility (face to face or virtual, as opportunities and resources dictate). This should be encouraged in all professions and sections in the health facility to allow cross-learning and strengthen teamwork.
- monitor client feedback on service provision by reviewing a complaint and compliment register and conducting exit interviews at least monthly. This should also include monitoring of disrespect, contempt and abuse in service provisions, thus promoting good conduct and people-centered care.

Step 2: Developing an Action Plan

The in-charge is required to address the identified shortfall using a plan of action indicating the set of activities to address the problem. The plan might include what will be done, when and the responsible person and the expected output as per the example indicated in Table 3.1. The in-charge should share and discuss the identified problem, possible causes and solutions with the health facility committee, health staff, and the health facility management committee. In addition, the in-charges should monitor the implementation of the action plan to know whether they lead to an improvement. The results of the monitoring should be shared with the health facility governing committee, facility quality improvement teams and Health Facility Management Teams.

TABLE 3.1 Action Plan for Improving Accountability and Transparency to Improve Health Service Delivery

PROBLEM	DESCRIPTION OF THE PROBLEM	POTENTIAL CAUSES OF THE PROBLEM	PROPOSED ACTIVITIES TO ADDRESS THE PROBLEM	RESPONSIBLE PERSON	DEADLINE FOR ADDRESSING THE PROBLEM
Corruption	Client was paying for services she was not supposed to pay for and paying directly to the doctor.	• Lack of directions at the health facility on where and how to pay	• Display costs of services and payment systems on the facility notice boards and units (including a big billboard at the entrance gate)	Health facility accountant (Juma Ali)	Within two weeks of developing an action plan
		• Lack of knowledge in the surrounding community on policies related to financing health services	• Provide community education on policies related to financing health services once a month in village/ community meetings	Health facility in-charge (Jane Felix)	Every month for a year
		• Lack of a corruption monitoring system at the health facility	• Prepare and implement a monthly corruption monitoring plan (exit interviews, suggestion box, text messages) in all departments and submit reports at monthly health facility management meeting	Heads of departments	Every month for a year
Lack of professionalism and ethics	The doctor performed a procedure that he/ she knew would not help the patient.	• Lack of CPD at the health facility	• Prepare and implement a weekly CPD plan per department	Heads of departments	Starting next week

(continued)

TABLE 3.1 *(Continued)*

PROBLEM	DESCRIPTION OF THE PROBLEM	POTENTIAL CAUSES OF THE PROBLEM	PROPOSED ACTIVITIES TO ADDRESS THE PROBLEM	RESPONSIBLE PERSON	DEADLINE FOR ADDRESSING THE PROBLEM
		• Lack of internal supportive supervision and quality assessment at the facility	• Conduct monthly internal supportive supervision and assessment for all departments at the facility	Chairperson of the quality improvement committee (Mwajuma Mawazo)	Every month, starting next month
Poor quality of services	The "usual" doctor did not refer a patient for further treatment and did not explain the problem the patient was suffering from.	• Lack of CPD • Lack of referral protocols at the facility (internal and external referrals)	• Prepare referral protocols (internal and external)	Nursing officer in-charge (Husna Jumbe)	In three weeks' time
	Not all patients were registered at the OPD	• Inadequate tracking system of patients in the medical records/ registration room	• Monitor new and reattending clients at the OPD	Nursing officer in charge of the OPD (Ally Juma)	Starting next week

Note: There is a need to identify areas that may require mentorship/capacity-building from high levels in service delivery, in this case:

1. Capacity-building for customer care, ethics and professionalism
2. Capacity-building for quality improvement

3.3 SCENARIO TWO

A 34-year-old woman, G6P5L4, who received her first antenatal care (ANC) visit at 18 weeks, completed four ANC visits at Kabatange Health Centre and used a "*bodaboda*" for transport from home to the health center, a commute of one hour. At 32 weeks, gestation age (GA) was admitted at Kabatange Health Centre with labor pain at around 3:00 pm; three hours later (6:00 pm), she delivered by spontaneous vaginal delivery (SVD) four babies weighing 1,500 gm, 1,000 gm, 900 gm, and 800 g. After the delivery health provider went home to rest, relatives started complaining and requesting a referral, which was then heard by calling an ambulance.

The mother and babies were kept in the delivery room for six hours postdelivery until when the ambulance arrived at around 11:00 pm; two hours later (1:00 am) they arrived at Kilimani A. Hospital. All this time, thermal care was poor, as the mother commented "*walipigwa na baridi sana, maana sikujua kama nitajifungua mtoto zaidi ya mmoja, nilikuja na nguo chache hazikutosha kuwafunika wote vizuri*", translated as: "they were very much exposed to the cold, I did not know I was going to deliver more than one baby, I had few clothes and they were not enough to cover all of them adequately".

On arrival at the hospital, one of them had died, the other three and mother were admitted to the Kangaroo Mother Care (KMC) room, but the mother mentioned that two of them were in critical condition. Mother was asked to keep the two babies in KMC care, and the relative was asked to keep one baby in the KMC position too. About 30 minutes later, the mother noticed the second baby had stopped breathing and was flabby. Within a short time, the third baby died too. Three weeks later, a team of NICU assessors arrived at the hospital and found only one baby alive, the one with an 800 g birth weight, weighing 930 g in the KMC room.

However, the quality of KMC care was inadequate, as there was no appropriate thermal care and throughout the stay. The baby has never been checked for hypoglycemia or infections, and vitamin K1 had never been given. It was the mother who told the team the story; there was no other documentation about this case scenario, no file, and even the perinatal forms for these cases were not available.

3.3.1 Consider these Questions

1. How applicable is this scenario to your facility?
2. What might be the cause of the governance challenges experienced in this scenario?

3. What are the roles of the in-charge of the health facility and the management team to address the governance challenges experienced in this scenario?
4. What could be looked at during internal supportive supervision at the health facility to address governance challenges?

3.3.2 Reflection

This scenario reminds us of leadership and governance in health service delivery at the facility and in the community. Specifically, the governance and leadership issues that guide reflection were, in this case, related to accountability, quality of care and professional obligations of the providers at the point of care. The scenario stipulates that the woman completed four ANC visits, but it looks like the ANC health workers did not detect a multiple pregnancy, or if they detected it, they did not take appropriate actions related to the plan of delivery. This points to the fact that the quality of ANC care in the facility or the outreach sites of the facility was poor and needed urgent intervention.

The fact that the healthcare worker disappeared after the woman delivered the four premature and low birth weight babies without giving proper care, such as keeping the babies warm and providing emergency referral, points out a serious problem of accountability and professionalism. It is noted that relatives complained and requested the referral, meaning that the healthcare worker was unwilling to provide a referral based on clinical assessment of the client or pressure from the relatives, although it was obvious that the babies and their mother needed emergency referral.

The absence of suitable infrastructure to keep the babies warm at the facility and proper medications also indicates poor planning by the management team. This points to accountability and lack of duty of care. The in-charge and the health facility workers have a legal obligation to adhere to a standard of reasonable care while performing their duties.

Moreover, the observation that the babies did not receive proper assessment and treatments (failure to check for hypoglycemia and infections and failure to give vitamin K) points to a possible lack of skills to handle the preterm/low birth weight babies, and also a possible lack of accountability and lack of duty of care among the health workers. Promoting CPD for all healthcare workers at the facility and ensuring the use of standards in service provision are leadership obligations of the facility in-charge and the management team.

3.3.3 Addressing the Problem and Developing an Action Plan

Step 1: Addressing the Problem

The governance and leadership issues in health service delivery presented in this scenario relate to transparency, accountability, responsiveness and quality of health services. To address these aspects of governance and leadership, the in-charges should:

(i) **Transparency**
  - share information on health facility performance with the public and promote transparency of quality measurements/assessment.
  - display publicly health services and their related costs on the health facility notice boards and in other areas.
  - inform the clients on the services available at the health facility.
  - display referral procedures on the facility notice boards.
  - inform clients to submit their complaints or complements in the case of dissatisfaction or satisfaction, respectively, with services provided at the health facility (provide a suggestion box at every health service provision site).
  - display the phone numbers of facility in-charge in the notice board.
  - conduct an exit interview whenever necessary to monitor service delivery.
  - manage complaints by addressing them immediately.
  - improve feedback mechanisms through a suggestion box, text messages, phone calls and exit interviews to reduce violence against patients and health workers.

(ii) **Accountability**
  - develop a comprehensive health facility plan to guide the improvement of health services.
  - create special rooms or wards for clients with insurance and fast-track services to improve health services.
  - allocate jobs effectively to health workers to ensure that care is provided to clients day and night.
  - monitor the performance of health workers in the health facility.
  - assess daily performance reports by collecting daily reports from all provision sites.
  - manage all referrals of clients according to health service guidelines.
  - conduct periodic reviews of workload versus the number of health workers available.

- periodically assess/measure quality of services by assessing adequacy and appropriateness of resources, processes of care, outputs of care, outcomes (including client satisfaction with care) of care and impacts of care to clients.
- share and use the findings obtained to improve quality of health services.
- conduct weekly CPD sessions at the health facility.
- allow cross-learning and strengthen teamwork in all professions and sections in the health facility.
- supply working tools like perinatal management forms and medical record files.
- promote continuous development of the knowledge, skills and abilities of staff by encouraging and rewarding innovation and supporting short and long courses.

(iii) **Responsiveness**
- publicly display the responsibilities and rights of both the clients and staff.
- ensure that the staff are familiar with what they are required to do.
- address issues raised in village/ward development committee and health facility governing committee meetings.

(iv) **Ethics**
- monitor professionalism and ethics in public services of all staff in the health facility.
- form a committee that will address professional conduct and ethics of health workers.
- take appropriate disciplinary actions with staff who do not abide by professional and ethical standards through the conduct and ethics committee of the health facility.

(v) **Rule of law**
- mobilize and actively disseminate key guidelines that guide the provision of health facilities.
- ensure that all staff provide care according to treatment guidelines and standard operating procedures.
- ensure that all referrals from the health facility are conducted according to agreed procedures and guidelines.

Step 2: Developing an Action Plan

The in-charge is required to address the identified shortfall using a plan of action indicating the set of activities to address the problem. The plan might include what will be done, when it will be done, the responsible person and the expected output, as per the example indicated in Table 3.2. The in-charge

TABLE 3.2 Action Plan for Improving the Quality of Maternal and Child Health Services to Improve Health Service Delivery at the Facility

PROBLEM	DESCRIPTION OF THE PROBLEM	POTENTIAL CAUSES OF THE PROBLEM	PROPOSED ACTIVITIES TO ADDRESS THE PROBLEM	RESPONSIBLE PERSON	DEADLINE FOR ADDRESSING THE PROBLEM
Poor quality of prenatal services	High-risk pregnancies were not detected in antenatal visits. The woman in the scenario was multiparous and had a multiple pregnancy.	• Lack of qualified personnel in antenatal clinics	• Reallocate personnel and make sure that the antenatal clinic has qualified personnel (registered nurses and midwives, dedicated clinicians)	Nursing officer in charge	Next week
		• Lack of guidelines and equipment	• Provide guidelines and equipment to the ANC clinic	Reproductive and Child Health (RCH) in-charge	Immediately
Poor quality of delivery services	Inappropriate care of the mother and babies at the health facility, including a lack of proper examination and management of the babies	• Lack of CPD at the health facility	• Prepare and implement a weekly CPD plan per department	Heads of departments	Starting next week
		• Lack of internal supportive supervision and quality assessment at the facility	• Conduct monthly internal supportive supervision and assessment to all departments at the facility	Chairperson of the quality improvement committee	Starting next month
		• Lack of patient treatment/nursing plans and partographs	• Supervise nursing care plans in all departments and partographs in the labor room of the facility	Nursing officer in charge	Starting next week

Note: The following areas may require mentorship/capacity-building from high levels in service delivery:
1. Orientation on some selected guidelines
2. Availability of clinical audit guides and checklists
3. Disciplinary guidance for staff who violate medical ethics or if there are conflicts at the health facility between the health facility workers

should share and discuss the identified problem, possible causes and solutions with the health facility committee and health staff. In addition, the in-charge should monitor the results of the action plan to know whether they lead to an improvement. The results of the monitoring should be shared with the health facility management teams, facility quality improvement teams and health facility governing committee.

3.3.4 Other Potential Issues

The proposed solutions based on the scenario aim to give an overview of how the leadership of a facility can address day-to-day challenges affecting the functioning of the health facility. It is important to note that issues presented in the scenario are not exhaustive. This chapter suggests that health facility in-charge and other HMT members should always consider other potential issues while executing their functions. Examples of other potential issues are presented in Box 3.1.

BOX 3.1   OTHER POTENTIAL ISSUES IN IMPROVING SERVICE DELIVERY

1. Working with the community: Cooperate with communities in improving and maintaining acceptable levels of healthcare.
2. Increasing health service coverage: Support community health workers and other community resource persons to extend service coverage beyond the health facility settings, that is, outreach services, community health education and promotion.
3. Providing infrastructure and equipment for service delivery: Construct and equip the service delivery units in the facility with infrastructure and equipment that enhances quality, equity and accountability. For example, you could check whether there are facilities for persons with disabilities—is the environment friendly to persons with disabilities? How are the toilets set? Are the buildings in general friendly to persons with disabilities? Is all equipment available at the service delivery points? How about daily stock of medicines and equipment?
4. Managing emergency cases: Establish a special task force to deal with emergencies and disasters at the health facility. This should also go hand-in-hand with developing a protocol on how to han-

dle emergency cases. For example, how is a person who has been assaulted and injured by other people handled at the hospital? How are power cuts handled at the hospital?

5. Monitoring patient satisfaction with services: Collect data on patient satisfaction with services through exit interviews, use of suggestion boxes and complaint and compliment bench (office). This will help to address quality issues for both clinical and non-clinical aspects in the health facility.

6. Managing the referral system: The facility management team should prepare a referral protocol (referral within the facility and outside the facility). This should stipulate who has to be notified such that all necessary resources for referral are mobilized, which resources are necessary for effective referral and what services need to be provided at the health facility and on the way. The in-charge of the health facility should have contact details (such as phone numbers) of all the nearby referral facilities and the district/regional medical officer for emergency contacts to facilitate smooth referral. Before referral, the in-charge should call the referral facility to inform them that there are patients who have been referred to their facility.

3.4 REFERENCES

Manzi, F., Schellenberg, J. A., Hutton, G., Wyss, K., Mbuya, C., Shirima, K., Mshinda, H., Tanner, M., & Schellenberg, D. (2012). Human resources for health care delivery in Tanzania: A multifaceted problem. *Human Resources for Health, 10*(1), 1–10.

Smith, P. C., Anell, A., Busse, R., Crivelli, L., Healy, J., Lindahl, A. K., Westert, G., & Kene, T. (2012). Leadership and governance in seven developed health systems. *Health Policy, 106*(1), 37–49.

World Health Organization (2007). *Everybody's business—strengthening health systems to improve health outcomes: WHO's framework for action.* World Health Organization. https://apps.who.int/iris/handle/10665/43918

World Health Organization (2010). *Monitoring the building blocks of health systems: A handbook of indicators and their measurement strategies.* World Health Organization. https://apps.who.int/iris/handle/10665/258734

Yip, W., Hafez, R., & World Health Organization (2015). *Improving health system efficiency: Reforms for improving the efficiency of health systems: Lessons from 10 country cases.* World Health Organization.

Health Workforce 4

Godfrey Kacholi and Mackfallen G. Anasel

Contents

4.1 INTRODUCTION

The health workforce is one of the major resources that play an important role in the success of health facilities and healthcare systems overall (Sirili et al., 2017; Guilbert, 2006). Therefore, proper management of human resources for health is of paramount importance for the health facility to deliver quality healthcare services while simultaneously improving patients' health outcomes. The World Health Organization defines the health workforce as all people engaged in actions whose primary intent is to enhance health. The health workforce is a combination of clinical staff, such as medical staff (physicians), nurses and midwives, and dentists, as well as allied health professionals such as dietitians, occupational therapists, pharmacists, physiotherapists (World Health Organization, 2006). The health workforce also includes management and support staff—who do not provide direct service but are important for the performance of the health facility, such as health managers,

DOI: 10.1201/9781003346821-4

ambulance drivers, laundry workers, security guards, electrical technicians and accountants.

Despite advancements in science and technology, the performance of any health facility depends mainly on the academic qualifications (knowledge), skills, and motivation of its health workforce for delivering quality health services (Sales et al., 2013). The first and foremost challenge that most health facilities are facing is the mismanagement of human resources for health. This challenge prevents health facilities from performing optimally, which can result in poor productivity, non-compliance with facility and national policies, demotivation and high staff turnover.

Sound leadership and governance capacity of the managers of health facilities is considered fundamental in developing, organizing and managing the health workforce to improve and sustain the performance of health facilities and ultimately contribute to improved health outcomes (Manzi et al., 2012). Leadership that complies with principles of good governance is key in tackling health workforce systematic challenges, such as shortages, distribution imbalances and employee skillset gaps (Dieleman & Hilhorst, 2010).

4.2 SCENARIO

The health facility in-charge of Gambacharo Health Centre, located in Gambacharo Ward, was invited to attend a three-day stakeholder meeting that involved eye health implementing partners at the regional level. On the sidelines of the stakeholders' meeting, the health facility in-charge requested one of the implementing partners to support Gambacharo Health Centre with optometry equipment to improve eye care services. The implementing partner showed interest in supporting the facility.

The health facility in-charge was asked by the implementing partner to prepare a financial proposal with a detailed list of optometry equipment and related supplies, including drugs needed. The facility in-charge was given a maximum of one week to submit the financial proposal for funding. The health facility in-charge, who had six months of working experience after completion of his medical internship, decided to lock himself in his office for two days to prepare the budget. He managed to submit the financial proposal to the funder within the given time. The facility in-charge was informally informed that the budget has been approved and that he would receive equipment and drugs within one week. He therefore made announcements to the general public that, starting from June 18th, all people with eye problems should visit the facility for eye screening and treatment.

Within one week, the funder delivered all of the optometry equipment and drugs requested to the health facility. The ophthalmic assistant, who was around at the time of delivery, hesitated to receive the equipment due to the fact that members of the health facility management team were not aware of this plan. Also, the health facility in-charge was not around, and he did not delegate his duties to any of the members of the health facility management team. After consulting the facility in-charge, the ophthalmic assistant received the equipment and drugs. However, the ophthalmic assistant noted that a phoropter, a slit lamp and a stool for the eye care practitioner were neither delivered nor in the delivery note. The ophthalmic assistant contacted the health facility in-charge for feedback about the missing items of what the ophthalmic assistant called "key equipment" in the delivery of eye care services. The facility in-charge shouted at the ophthalmic assistant, saying *"your job is to receive and keep in the store, and that's what I instructed you to do"*. However, the facility in-charge contacted the funder to request the missing equipment and was informed that there was no additional budget.

The ophthalmic assistant was unhappy with the decisions made by his boss. When the facility in-charge discovered that the ophthalmic assistant was complaining to other staff about his decisions, the relationship between the two began to deteriorate day by day. This led some other staff in the facility to be on the side of the ophthalmic assistant; hence, the facility in-charge began to lose cooperation from his subordinates.

The District Medical Officer (DMO) visited Gambacharo Health Centre three weeks after the postponed scheduled visit. At the health facility, this was a surprise visit. Meanwhile, all of the people with eye problems who had been informed about the availability of eye care services from the aforementioned date had arrived at the facility. The DMO was very surprised to see that the facility was overcrowded at the reception, and patients were complaining bitterly. The DMO went straight to the staff at the reception. He introduced himself to the staff at reception and asked why there was overcrowding. He wanted more from the answers given at the reception. Immediately, the facility in-charge came to the reception after being informed that the DMO had come. The DMO asked the in-charge why there was overcrowding. The facility in-charge narrated the whole story. The DMO decided to inspect the facility store to see the eye equipment and drugs supplied by the partner without his knowledge. However, at that time, nobody knew where the keys were kept. The DMO decided to get in his car and return to his office.

Three days later, the council health management team (CHMT), under the leadership of the DMO, visited Gambacharo Health Centre. This time, the DMO informed the facility in-charge about their visit; the proposed time of arrival was 14:00 hours. Ideally, the CHMT wanted to have a meeting with facility staff, including an inspection of the facility when patient and client inflow was minimal. Facility staff were asked to openly share their own working experiences and challenges they were facing, and to propose what should be improved. During the meeting, some staff complained that most of the time, the facility in-charge worked alone with an assumption that he was more knowledgeable than anyone at the health facility; this included performing activities that are out of his profession. One staff member, who had been working in the facility for the past two years, reported to the CHMT that even mid-year staff performance reviews were not conducted, and there were no plans to conduct annual performance appraisals for the ending year.

The CHMT, under the leadership of DMO, collected all opinions from the facility staff. The DMO thanked the staff on behalf of the CHMT and promised to address their concerns as soon as possible. Then, the CHMT had a brief meeting with the facility in-charge to get some clarifications on some of the issues.

4.2.1 Consider these Questions

1. What is your own experience in relation to this scenario?
2. What are the major health workforce leadership and governance issues that the scenario is trying to portray?
3. What do you propose should be done to improve health workforce leadership and governance-related issues in the health facility?
4. How can supportive supervision, mentorship and coaching to the facility health workforce by the higher-level authorities improve the performance of health facilities?

4.2.2 Reflection

The scenario aims to remind us of the importance of participation, transparency, accountability, adherence to rules and procedures and inclusion of the health workforce in the planning, budgeting and implementation processes of various activities of health facilities. The scenario underscores how poor leadership and governance can cause frustration, affect staff morale and ultimately affect the performance of health facilities and health outcomes.

4.2.3 Addressing the Problem and Developing an Action Plan

Step 1: Addressing the Problem

To improve governance-associated elements such as adherence to rule of law, insurance of transparency, promotion of accountability and active participation and engagement of the health workforce; the health facility in-charge should observe the following aspects:

(i) **Rule of law**
- Entering into contractual agreements or partnerships with implementing partners, voluntary organizations or any other public or non-public organizations in accordance with the government procedures and regulations.
- Conducting staff performance appraisals according to the set procedures.
- Adhering to the rules, guidelines, laws, standard operational procedures and protocols.
- Delegation and separation of power/division of labor.

(ii) **Transparency**
- Involving the health workforce in health facility planning, budgeting, implementation and reporting processes as early as possible:
  - Providing them with a planning schedule and what you expect from them.
  - Orienting them on the importance of planning and budgeting.
  - Conducting hands-on training on how planning and budgeting are carried out.
  - Supporting them (technically) to develop plans and budgets for their units/sections.
  - Encouraging teamwork during planning and budgeting, and reporting processes by assigning tasks to each staff member.
- Communicating all contractual agreements or any support received from within or outside of the government system through relevant authorities:
  - Becoming familiar with the available procedures and regulations that guide contractual agreements.
  - Sharing and agreeing with the facility management team before entering into any contractual agreement or accepting any support.

- Consulting relevant authorities about the envisioned contracts, agreements or any support to be received for guidance and approval.
- Keeping the contractual agreements in safe custody for future reference and retrieval.
- Using formal reporting structures for communication and coordination within and across levels of the health facility.

(iii) **Participation**
- Embracing the use of formal meetings to decide which are the most serious problems or priorities in the facility and what can be done to address them:
  - Preparing and disseminating meeting schedules with staff in a timely manner.
  - Developing agendas and share with staff and frequently collecting issues from staff to guide the preparation of agendas.
  - Setting the date, time and venue for the meetings; these should be formally communicated in advance.
  - Asking everyone to freely contribute during the meeting.
  - Managing time but being flexible to enhance participation.
  - Documenting minutes for future reference and follow-up.
  - Developing practices of making follow-ups on the issues agreed upon in the meetings.
- Developing a relaxed working climate for the health workforce to share ideas, innovations and expectations:
  - Accommodating ideas of every staff member.
  - Recognizing hard workers by announcing them in different meetings and notice boards, and providing them with recognition letters.
  - Showing trust to each staff member.
  - Involving staff in planning time for fun and enjoyment.
  - Being a role model (trusted and respected) at the workplace.
  - Participating in social events such as weddings, funerals and other ceremonies of staff and their families.
- Improving interpersonal relationships among health facility staff, especially between the facility management and staff:
  - Controlling emotions of staff and yourself (in-charge).
  - Developing a culture of respecting and recognizing others' experiences and expertise.
  - Being active listeners and encouraging staff to be resilient to each other.

- Avoiding treating staff as inhuman.
- Providing time for staff to do their job without unnecessary interference.
- Discouraging practices of spreading baseless rumours by encouraging open discussion through meetings.
- Passing on correct and reliable information to staff using formal channels.
- Avoiding the use of harsh language with staff.
- Enhancing mutual trust, understanding and cooperation among staff in the health facility:
  - Always telling staff the truth and encouraging staff to do so.
  - Not hesitating to admit when you are wrong.
  - Explaining to staff your thoughts and asking them to share their ideas.
  - Taking responsibility for the failure while avoiding blaming your staff.
- Providing staff with informational updates on policies or new recommended practices:
  - Communicating with relevant authorities to learn about new policies or guidelines.
  - Collecting the policies and guidelines.
  - Taking time to read and understand new guidelines and policies.
  - Disseminating the new policies and guidelines to staff by having dissemination sessions.
  - Following up to learn if staff are complying with the guidelines.
- Sharing and discussing expectations, challenges and recommendations of the staff with the health facility management team:
  - Guiding the facility management team to identify areas of strength and weakness; these should be objective.
  - Leading the facility management team to develop strategies to solve identified problems.
  - Providing constructive feedback to individual staff members and, where necessary, to all staff through scheduled staff meetings.
  - Always remembering to address challenges collectively.
  - Leading the facility management team and individual staff members to set their targets and strategies for improvement.

(iv) **Accountability**
- Preparing job descriptions that describe clearly the roles and responsibilities of each health facility staff member in accordance with their professions.
- Providing a basis for rewarding staff in relation to their contribution to health facility goals:
  - Using the available performance appraisal system to identify high-performing employees.
  - Involving staff to determine criteria for rewarding facility staff.
  - Giving awards openly.
- Applying agreed-upon work standards of performance and specifying the procedures for the appraisal of staff performance.
- Identifying staff that need specific training for one or other aspect of their work.
- Conducting timely performance appraisal.
- Establishing a disciplinary committee to deal with misconduct of staff.
- As a leader, protecting your staff against external interference.

Step 2: Developing an Action Plan

After problem analysis, the in-charge is required to address the identified shortfall using the correct measures. In order to address the identified challenges genuinely, the health facility in-charge is expected to involve staff from each unit, section and department to identify potential challenges and collectively suggest the possible solutions. The identified challenges must be put into an action plan for operationalization. An example of the action plan is indicated in Table 4.1.

4.2.4 Other Potential Issues

The proposed solutions based on the scenario aim to give an overview of how the leadership of a facility can address day-to-day challenges affecting the functioning of the health facilities. It is important to note that issues presented in the scenario are not exhaustive. This chapter suggests that health facilities in-charge and other HMT members should always consider other potential issues while executing their functions. Examples of other potential issues are presented in Box 4.1.

TABLE 4.1 An Action Plan for Managing the Health Workforce

PROBLEM	DESCRIPTION OF THE PROBLEM	POTENTIAL CAUSES OF THE PROBLEM	PROPOSED ACTIVITIES TO ADDRESS THE PROBLEM	RESPONSIBLE PERSON	DEADLINE OF ADDRESSING THE PROBLEM
Transparency	Staff with relevant professions and experience in eye health were not involved in the planning and budgeting process.	• Lack of trust in subordinates • Subordinates have no interest	• Enhance mutual trust, understanding and cooperation among staff in the health facility • Prepare job descriptions that describe clearly the roles and responsibilities of each health facility staff member in accordance with their professions and jobs	Medical officer in charge (MoI)	Two weeks after preparation of the action plan
		• The storekeeper was not around and keys could not be found	• Develop procedures and practices for delegation and hand-over		Immediately
Participation	Staff had no opportunity to share their feelings; hence, rumors were inevitable	• No formal meetings were conducted for sharing	• Embrace the use of formal meetings to ensure that staff are well-informed	Health facility secretary	Having quarterly facility meetings
Keys for the store were not available	The storekeeper was not around and keys could not be found	• Challenges related to delegation and office hand-over	• Develop procedures and practices for delegation and hand-over	MoI	Immediately

BOX 4.1   OTHER POTENTIAL ISSUES IN MANAGING THE HEALTH WORKFORCE

1. Conducting workload analysis to identify staff shortages and surplus within the facility: Use the workload analysis results to plan for task shifting and task sharing. Ensure proper allocation and replacement of staff.

2. Using available performance management systems such as OPRAS to improve the performance of the health workforce at the facility: Distribute each staff member with a clear and detailed job description. Regularly, make sure that tasks as indicated in the job description of each staff are performed. Use OPRAS and other easy and cheap methods to conduct training needs assessments of health facility staff—this should be done annually.

3. Establishing staff motivation and retention mechanisms (may not necessarily be financial): Show new and old staff that you trust them by giving them responsibilities that enable them to grow. Respect and appreciate staff regardless of their positions. Provide financial rewards (if available) and non-financial rewards such as letters of appreciation and recognition for their performance. Provide on-going mentorship support. Create professional development opportunities such as attending short and long courses. Provide staff with working space and tools needed for their jobs. Manage conflicts timely and use the appropriate disciplinary measures and structures. Facilitate the payment of statutory benefits and motivation to staff.

4. Conducting staff meetings in accordance with the laws and regulations: Use appropriate, credible and approved channels of communication to convey messages to staff and other relevant authorities. Prepare meeting agendas, dates, and venues; write minutes.

5. Improving interpersonal relationships by creating feedback mechanisms: Conduct staff induction and orientation for new staff, including staff assuming new roles and responsibilities in the facility (use available staff induction guidelines if need be). Prepare and give new staff a tour to all places and offices at the workplace. Introduce new staff to all supervisors and to all staff in the facility. Give them all necessary equipment and working space for them to start working. Tell new staff about important rules and procedures that should be observed. Attach them to specific staff members, such as seniors, for mentorship and back-up during the orientation period (if need be) and make a follow-up.

6. Conducting internal supportive supervision to units, structures (QIT, WITs), wards and non-clinical services within the facility: Plan and arrange for supportive supervision, focusing on coaching and mentoring. Provide supportive supervision feedback—both written and oral.

7. Make use of volunteers: Define why you need them (volunteers) and follow procedures of engaging them. Provide them with excellent induction. Make the volunteers feel part of the working team by giving them basic support such as working space, tools, and opportunities to show their innovations. Establish good communication and trust between them and the available staff. Make sure that they are respected and appreciated to make them feel needed.

8. Professional ethics: Use public address (PA) systems to educate the clients and patients on corruption and how to report it in the facility and to higher authorities.

4.3 REFERENCES

Dieleman, D., & Hilhorst, T. (2010). *Improving human resources for health: Turning attention to governance Amsterdam.* Royal Tropical Institute (KIT).

Guilbert, J. J. (2006). The world health report 2006: Working together for health. *Education for Health (Abingdon, England), 19*(3), 385–387. https://doi.org/10.1080/13576280600937911

Manzi, F., Schellenberg, J. A., Hutton, G., Wyss, K., Mbuya, C., Shirima, K., Mshinda, H., Tanner, M., & Schellenberg, D. (2012). Human resources for health care delivery in Tanzania: A multifaceted problem. *Human Resources for Health, 10*(1), 1–10.

Sales, M., Kieny, M. P., Krech, R., & Etienne, C. (2013). Human resources for universal health coverage: From evidence to policy and action. In *Bulletin of the world health organization* (Vol. 91, pp. 798–798A). SciELO Public Health.

Sirili, N., Kiwara, A., Gasto, F., Goicolea, I., & Hurtig, A. K. (2017). Training and deployment of medical doctors in Tanzania post-1990s health sector reforms: Assessing the achievements. *Human Resources for Health, 15*(1), 27. https://doi.org/10.1186/s12960-017-0202-7

World Health Organization (2006). *The world health report 2006: Working together for health.* World Health Organization.

Health Information Systems 5

Mackfallen G. Anasel and
Godfrey Kacholi

Contents

5.1 INTRODUCTION

Sound and reliable information systems, as stated by the WHO, are the foundation of leadership and governance in the health sector. Health information systems have four key functions: (1) data generation, (2) data compilation, (3) data analysis and synthesis and (4) data communication and use. In addition to being essential for monitoring and evaluation, health information systems serve to provide alerts and early warnings, support patients and health facility management, enable planning, stimulate research, permit situation and trend analyses and reinforce health changes for diverse users (World Health

Organization, 2018). Essentially, governance and leadership are of paramount importance in ensuring that accessible, high-quality health data is produced through health information management systems in accordance with the transparency and accountability principles of the health systems.

5.2 CULTURE OF DATA USE

Despite having health information systems that have the capability of data analysis, previous studies (Anasel et al., 2019; Ikonje, 2014; Nutley & Li, n.d.) indicate that the collected data is rarely analyzed and used for informed decision making, especially at lower levels of the health system where frontline health workers such as nurses and clinical officers are responsible for data-related tasks and service delivery (Hamad, 2019). The staff needs soft skills to access, analyze and interpret data for decision making at the facility, district, and national levels. There is a significant relationship between the availability of health information systems and data use (Seid et al., 2021). Also, it is assumed that data systems available within healthcare units are used to guide every decision made, action taken, and change made in that health unit and influenced by outside policies, norms and regulations (Heywood & Rohde, 2001). However, it was noted that in a study conducted by the Japan International Cooperation Agency (JICA) in collaboration with MOH that among 28 Regional Referral Hospitals (RRHs) in which human resources health information system (HRHIS) and health management information system (HMIS) were implemented; 16 (57.1%) and 11 (39.3%) hospitals were not updating and not using data, respectively. These systems have data visualization and data sharing capabilities, which facilitate data use for informed decision making. Despite the availability of HMIS, the JICA report further showed that 8 (28.6%) hospitals did not have systems for tracking medical errors. This shows the need of imparting a culture of data use along with an emphasis on improving data systems to support data usage. This is according to Heywood and Rohde (2001), who argue that information use is made easier if is ritualized and routines are set up as part of the "information culture".

Data use at the national and subnational levels is highly influenced by leadership and governance between those who produce data and those who use data for informed decisions. In Tanzania, there is limited interaction between health service providers (those who produce data) and managers (those who use data) to make decisions. This affects the whole chain of data flow from data collection to synthesis, analysis, interpretation and use. Data producers in facilities are often ignored by those making decisions and make assumptions about perceived information needs and incentives for acting on data, resulting in data generated without local relevance or practical utility (Darcy et al., 2017; Matee et al., 2017). They also have limited knowledge of leadership, decision-making cycles, strategic priorities and plans based on data generated at the facility by health information systems.

5.3 LEADERSHIP AND GOVERNANCE IN HEALTH INFORMATION SYSTEMS

Leadership and governance have long been underscored as keys to improving performance in the health sector. The interplay between leadership and governance and health information systems is critical for health planning processes, local health service accountability mechanisms, availability of information on provider performance, clarity of health sector legislation, enforcement of health regulations and availability of procedures to report misuse of resources (Fryatt et al., 2017). The health information system (HIS) is a service delivery engine whereby health data are recorded, stored, retrieved and processed for informed decision-making (Krishnan et al., 2010; World Health Organization, 2010). The HIS is one of the six core building blocks of the health system and provides data needed for other components (World Health Organization, 2010). Data delivered through the HIS come from service delivery reports and administrative records kept as part of routine transactions at health facilities and management offices. Leadership and governance of the HIS is an important element that ensures the data collected are processed and transformed, communicated and used to improve decisions toward improved health outcomes.

It is important to remember that the health information system is crucial to inform facility management teams of the status of health services in the facility (Endriyas et al., 2019; Mutale et al., 2013). The facility requires data to make informed decisions related to different levels of data collection, such as:

- individual level data relevant for clinical decision making, patient tracking, etc.
- health facility data, such as procurement records and staff performance, which enables managers to determine resource needs.

- community level data; for example, household surveys are useful for public health decision making, since they include both service users and non-users.
- surveillance data focusing on defining problems and providing a timely basis for action, for example in epidemic response.

In addition, it has been recognized that governance and HIS have been identified as key, interacting levers of health system strengthening (De Savigny & Adam, 2009; Scott & Gilson, 2017). The HIS, meanwhile, is commonly understood as a tool of governance used in decision-making and allowing oversight of resources deployed and outcomes achieved (World Health Organization, 2008). There has, therefore, been considerable focus on and investment in HISs for health system strengthening in resource-limited countries to enhance the governance of health service delivery (AbouZahr & Boerma, 2005; Shakarishvili et al., 2010; Stansfield et al., 2011; World Health Organization, 2007).

This chapter aims to vividly demonstrate the application of leadership and governance in ensuring the collection of quality data and the analysis and use of said data. The essential element of leadership and governance presented in this chapter is accountability.

5.4 SCENARIO

On October 30th, 2020, the CHMT visited Maekani Health Centre for normal supportive supervision. Upon arrival at the OPD, they found a long queue of clients and patients waiting for services from the clinician while complaining that they were not given services on time. One patient clarified that they had waited for a long time without getting the services.

The CHMT noted that only two doctors' rooms out of five had clinicians. The team decided to investigate the possible causes for the observed shortfall. The team obtained the list of the clinicians available at the facility and the ones allocated to the OPD. The facility had seven (7) clinicians, including one medical doctor, three AMOs, and three clinical officers. It was also noted that five clinicians were allocated to the OPD on the day of supervision; two clinicians were absent and one was in the laboratory chatting with laboratory staff.

TABLE 5.1   Recorded Data in the MTUHA Book 5/GoTHOMIS

CLINICIAN	PATIENT REGISTER (N)	TALLY (N)	SUMMARY & DHIS2 (N)	DISCREPANCIES (N)
1	988	1024	1024	+ 36
2	512	497	497	- 15
3	400	723	723	+ 323
4	220	102	102	- 118
5	152	125	125	- 27
6	436	435	435	- 1
7	105	78	78	- 27

Note: In normal situations, the data at the OPD are expected to be higher than those at the laboratory. Likewise, in the facility that has an IPD, the data of the OPD plus that of the IPD must be greater or the same as the data at the Laboratory.

The team decided to conduct a vigorous analysis of the case to identify whether there were issues to be addressed. The number of patients saved for the last month was assessed and the result was shocking. The monthly summary book and DHIS 2 indicated that the OPD served 2,984 patients with different illnesses, while the laboratory data indicated 3,987 patients who were tested. This information triggered the team to do a further assessment to identify the daily performance of each clinician. The GoTHOMIS/MTUHA Book 5, which includes patients' registers, tally sheets, and summary books, were examined. Again, the data indicated discrepancies between patients' registers and tally sheets for the seven clinicians as indicated in Table 5.1.

5.4.1 Consider these Questions

1. How does this scenario apply to your facility?
2. Why do some clinicians not report each patient/client after providing services?
3. How can this problem be addressed?

5.4.2 Reflection

Poor reporting of OPD data in GoTHOMIS/MTUHA Book 5 is a serious problem observed in the scenario. Poor OPD records at Maekani Health Centre may lead to inadequate fund disbursement because the available data in

DHIS 2 indicated few clients. The scenario indicates that the data of clients and patients who attend the OPD are underreported, which suggests a lack of accountability.

5.4.3 Addressing the Problem and Developing an Action Plan

Step 1: Addressing the Problem

(i) **Accountability**
  - Conduct regular meetings with the OPD in-charge to discuss filling of MTUHA 5/GoTHOMIS and correctness of collected data. Document the meeting for follow up and future reference.
  - Execute internal facility disciplinary measures that include writing warning letters to staff who repeatedly fail to fill in the data in MTUHA/GoTHOMIS.
  - Ensure that MTUHA Book 5 is available and used by each clinician to record all clients/patents attended.
  - Ensure that GoTHOMIS is functional and follow up to ensure that all health service provision points are connected.
  - Ensure that the OPD staff roster is fairly distributed among the staff.
  - Conduct daily monitoring of the performance of each staff member by evaluating the number of patients/clients attended based on GoTHOMIS/MTUHA individual data.
  - Organize and facilitate job training/refresher courses on health information management systems, especially for new employees.
  - Ensure that each staff member provides data on daily performance.
  - Ensure that the department/section conducts daily spots and cross-checks the correctness of the data.
  - Ensure that the QIT conducts monthly data review meetings; reflect on the numbers that are collected daily in the facility and share the review findings with the HMT.
  - Conduct DQA and data triangulation from different sources in the facility to assess whether they convey the same message on a quarterly basis.

- Supervise the smooth running of GoTHOMIS and other software and systems available at facility, such as FFARS, PlanRep and eLMIS.
- Analyze and discuss the data at the facility level before submitting them to a higher authority.
- Use and disseminate data by displaying them on each department/section notice board in accordance with national indicators. Ideally, the display should be in the form of a bar chart for comparison and a line graph showing the trend over time.
- Make use of available data to inform evidence-based decisions related to facility operations such as staff allocation, planning and budgeting.
- Inform the staff of the link between budget allocation at the facility and accurate data.
- Seek technical assistance from the HMIS Coordinator and CHMT regarding any issue related to HISs.

Step 2: Developing an Action Plan

The facility in-charge is required to lead the HMT to prepare an action plan to address the identified shortfalls. The plan should include the activity, time frame, responsible person and the expected results, as indicated in Table 5.2. The facility in-charge should share and discuss the identified problem, possible causes and the action plan with the OPD staff and other departments/sections for learning and improvement. This will be followed by monitoring of the changes in data reporting. The accountability of individual staff members at health facilities should be strengthened to ensure that complete, accurate and quality data are generated for informed decisions.

5.4.4 Other Potential Issues

The proposed solutions based on the scenario aim to give an overview of how the leadership of the facility can address day-to-day challenges affecting the functioning of the health facility. It is important to note that the issues presented in the scenario are not exhaustive. This chapter suggests that health facility in-charge and other HMT members should always consider other potential issues while executing their functions. Examples of other potential issues are presented in Box 5.1.

TABLE 5.2 Action Plan for Addressing Absenteeism and Data Collection/Reporting

PROBLEM	DESCRIPTION OF THE PROBLEM	POTENTIAL CAUSES OF THE PROBLEM	PROPOSED ACTIVITIES TO ADDRESS THE PROBLEM	RESPONSIBLE PERSON	DEADLINE OF ADDRESSING THE PROBLEM
Poor quality of the collected and reported data	The scenario indicates underreporting of OPD data. There is a discrepancy in data from different sources.	• Not knowing the importance of data • Lack of culture to collect and make use of data • Misconception that the data are collected for high levels and not for them to use • Poor documentation • Increased workload due absenteeism of some staff	• Cross-check the data quality and accuracy by assessing different points for data collection • Analyze the report of MTUHA Book 5/ GoTHOMIS and other systems available at facility • Check and document the number of clients attended by each clinician and share the reports with the staff • Highlight the sources of the discrepancies observed and share with the staff • Inform the clinician of the importance of recording the patients/clients' medical records after consultation • Create a plan for regular follow-up to ascertain whether the observed shortfalls have been addressed • Identify staff who were absent from their working station • Check if they have official permission • Identify the average number of days they have been outside of the working station • Remember, if the staff has spent more than fourteen days on private issues, they should be deducted from his/her monthly leave	Facility in-charge and HS	Two weeks from the date action plan has been proposed

**BOX 5.1   OTHER POTENTIAL ISSUES TO CONSIDER
IN HEALTH INFORMATION SYSTEMS**

1. Working with the community: Sensitize community members to report household and community data such as people with disability, home deliveries and deaths, children, elders and pregnant women. Involve the village council, health facility governing committee and community health workers to collect the community data as a requirement of the facility budgeting process.
2. Increasing health service coverage: Use data to understand health service coverage for different groups such elders, people with disabilities and indigents. Use data to plan for other services to be provided at the facility, such as ultrasound services, delivery services and IPD services. Use findings from assessments, evaluation reports and research to improve the services provisions.
3. Conducting operational research.
4. Ensuring data protection.
5. Ensuring accurate collection of vitals registration (birth and death data) and report to relevant authorities in a timely manner.

5.5 REFERENCES

AbouZahr, C., & Boerma, T. (2005). Health information systems: The foundations of public health. *Bulletin of the World Health Organization, 83*(8), 578–583.

Anasel, M. G., Swai, I. L., & Masue, O. S. (2019). *Creating a culture of data use in Tanzania: Assessing health providers' capacity to analyze and use family planning data.* MEASURE Evaluation.

Darcy, N. M., Somi, G., Matee, M., Wengaa, D., & Perera, S. (2017). Data dissemination and use (DDU) strategy development: Design of the DDU strategy methodology. *Journal of Health Informatics in Africa, 4*(1).

De Savigny, D., & Adam, T. (2009). *Systems thinking for health systems strengthening.* World Health Organization.

Endriyas, M., Alano, A., Mekonnen, E., Ayele, S., Kelaye, T., Shiferaw, M., Misganaw, T., Samuel, T., Hailemariam, T., & Hailu, S. (2019). Understanding performance data: Health management information system data accuracy in Southern nations nationalities and people's region, Ethiopia. *BMC Health Services Research, 19*(1), 1–6.

Fryatt, R., Bennett, S., & Soucat, A. (2017). Health sector governance: Should we be investing more? *BMJ Global Health, 2*(2), e000343. https://doi.org/10.1136/bmjgh-2017-000343

Hamad, W. B. (2019). Current position and challenges of e-health in Tanzania: A review of literature. *Global Scientific Journal, 7*(9).

Heywood, A., & Rohde, J. (2001). *Using information for action: A manual for health workers at facility level.* The Equity Project.

Ikonje, A. (2014). *Strengthening data management and use in decision making to improve health care services: Lessons learnt.* University Research Co. LLC (URC).

Krishnan, A., Nongkynrih, B., Yadav, K., Singh, S., & Gupta, V. (2010). Evaluation of computerized health management information system for primary health care in rural India. *BMC Health Services Research, 10*(1), 1–13.

Matee, M. I., Somi, G., Wengaa, D., Darcy, N., & Perera, S. (2017). Data dissemination and use (DDU) strategy development: Design of the DDU strategy methodology. *Journal of Health Informatics in Africa, 4*(1).

Mutale, W., Chintu, N., Amoroso, C., Awoonor-Williams, K., Phillips, J., Baynes, C., Michel, C., Taylor, A., & Sherr, K. (2013). Improving health information systems for decision making across five sub-Saharan African countries: Implementation strategies from the African health initiative. *BMC Health Services Research, 13*(2), 1–12.

Nutley, T., & Li, M. (n.d.). *Conceptualizing and measuring data use: A review of assessments and tools.* Retrieved June 2018, from https://www.Measureevaluation.Org/Resources/Publications/Wp-18-214

Scott, V., & Gilson, L. (2017). Exploring how different modes of governance act across health system levels to influence primary healthcare facility managers' use of information in decision-making: Experience from Cape Town, South Africa. *International Journal for Equity in Health, 16*(1), 1–15.

Seid, M. A., Bayou, N. B., Ayele, F. Y., & Zerga, A. A. (2021). Utilization of routine health information from health management information system and associated factors among health workers at health centers in Oromia special zone, Ethiopia: A multilevel analysis. *Risk Management and Healthcare Policy, 14,* 1189.

Shakarishvili, G., Atun, R., Berman, P., Hsiao, W., Burgess, C., & Lansang, M. A. (2010). Converging health systems frameworks: Towards a concepts-to-actions roadmap for health systems strengthening in low and middle income countries. *Global Health Governance, 3*(2).

Stansfield, S. K., Walsh, J., Prata, N., & Evans, T. (2011). *Information to improve decision making for health.* 2nd ed. World Bank. PMID: 21250312.

World Health Organization (2007). *Everybody's business—strengthening health systems to improve health outcomes: WHO's framework for action.* World Health Organization. https://apps.who.int/iris/handle/10665/43918.

World Health Organization (2008). *Toolkit on monitoring health systems strengthening health information systems.* World Health Organization.

World Health Organization (2010). *Monitoring the building blocks of health systems: A handbook of indicators and their measurement strategies.* World Health Organization. https://apps.who.int/iris/handle/10665/258734.

World Health Organization (2018). Analysis and use of health facility data: General principles. *Health statistics and information systems.* https://www.who.int/healthinfo/FacilityAnalysis_GeneralPrinciples.pdf?ua=1

Health Commodities and Technologies

6

Mackfallen G. Anasel and Albino Kalolo

Contents

6.1 INTRODUCTION

Leadership and governance ensure that policy and legal framework, structures, and systems for organizing, financing and regulating the system and facilitating coordination, participation and accountability are established

DOI: 10.1201/9781003346821-6

and enforced (MSH, 2017; Rauscher et al., 2018). Governance and leadership practices in primary health facilities play a significant role in the constant availability of essential health commodities (medicines, medical supplies and equipment) and technologies for effective service delivery (Kuwawenaruwa et al., 2020). The availability of quality medicines in the provision at primary health facilities is an integral part of universal health coverage (UHC) (Prinja et al., 2016). Evidence suggests that the availability of medicines is essential for healthcare service delivery (Bigdeli et al., 2015; Obare et al., 2014).

Leadership and governance practices are vital for a well-functioning health system that is envisaged to ensure equitable and sustainable access to essential medical products, vaccines and technologies whilst ensuring high quality of service, safety and affordable healthcare-related costs (Atif et al., 2019). The availability of health commodities and technologies in health facilities is challenged by such factors as inadequate funding, weak supply chain management, shortage of pharmaceutical personnel, suboptimal rationing of medicines and rapid change in diagnostic technologies, which could be addressed by good governance and leadership practices (Cameron et al., 2009; Yadav, 2015).

6.2 GOVERNANCE AND LEADERSHIP IN HEALTH COMMODITIES AND TECHNOLOGIES

Good governance and leadership at the health facility level are essential for an effective supply chain system and management of medicines, vaccines and other essential health commodities and technologies. Managers of health facilities have a role to play to ensure effective planning and forecasting, procurement, storage and use of health commodities. When leadership and governance are ignored, it attracts corruption, diverts government resources and jeopardizes the quality of services provided. The potential for corruption exists in all levels of health systems. This could be collusion in the procurement process, price-fixing of supplies, and leakages or diversion in the distribution chain. Proper management of health commodities helps to minimize waste of commodities, thus preventing stockouts at the health facility and its units or departments.

This chapter focuses on health commodities and technologies. Governance and leadership elements that are important in addressing availability of health commodities in health facilities are presented and include transparency, accountability, equity and inclusiveness and participation.

6.3 SCENARIO ONE

Mr. Mabula and his wife Koku are farmers and have two children, Lwiza (daughter) and Levi (son). Mr. Mabula's family lives in Nkana, which is one of the villages in the catchment area of the Nkana Health Centre. The family lives 10 km away from the health center. One day, Lwiza had a high fever and was carried to the health facility by her father using a bicycle. Mr. Mabula explained to the attending clinician at the facility that his daughter had been with a fever for the past seven days. The clinician ordered a rapid test for malaria (mRDT), which showed that Lwiza had malaria. The clinician prescribed an antipyretic (paracetamol) and an antimalarial (artemether lumefantrine [ALu]) for Lwiza. Thereafter, the clinician directed Mr. Mabula to go to the facility pharmacy to collect the medicines. At the pharmacy, the medicine dispenser told Mr. Mabula that antimalarials were out of stock, and only paracetamol (a blister pack) was available. The dispenser advised Mr. Mabula to find medicine at a private medicine outlet (duka la dawa muhimu), where he could buy ALu. However, in the entire Nkana village there was no private medicine outlet around, so Mr. Mabula was left with no other option than taking Lwiza home with only paracetamol.

The following night, Lwiza's condition worsened, so Mr. Mabula decided to take her back to the health facility and told the clinician that he did not find ALu and his daughter was seriously sick. During that time, the facility in-charge referred Lwiza to Kanazi District Hospital, which is 40 km from Nkana, and called an ambulance from the district hospital to come and pick Lwiza, as she was seriously ill. One hour later, an ambulance arrived and the journey to the district hospital started. Upon arrival at the hospital, Lwiza was admitted, received investigation, and was diagnosed with malaria with severe anemia. A blood grouping and compatibility test was done, and found that she was blood group A positive. The doctor also found that the medicine (paracetamol) that was given to Lwiza at the health center had expired a month ago.

The doctor told Mr. Mabula that there was no blood to transfuse Lwiza, as it was out of stock. While Mr. Mabula was searching for a relative to donate, John, a CHMT member who came for supervision at the district hospital and heard Lwiza's story, decided to donate blood. Surprisingly, the laboratory technician told him that there were a few blood bottles left in the blood bank, so they would transfuse Lwiza.

Mabula's incident made the CHMT members follow up with both the district hospital and Nkana Health Centre. In their assessment, they found serious problems in planning, procurement, storage and use of health commodities. Specifically, for Nkana Health Center, they found that Asha, a medicine dispenser, had very little knowledge of the management of health commodities.

6.3.1 Consider these Questions

1. To what extent is the scenario relevant to your situation?
2. What problems can be highlighted in this scenario?
3. What might be the possible causes of the problems experienced in the scenario?
4. What can be done to address the identified problems?

6.3.2 Reflection

The scenario shows the challenges encountered by patients to get medicine at the point of care. The whole scenario delineates the issues associated with poor leadership and governance, manifested as poor planning and procurement of health commodities. Transparency, accountability, equity and inclusiveness and participation in management of medicine and equipment were lacking, causing the health facilities to have frequent stockouts of essential medicines. For example, it was not clear why the laboratory personnel didn't give blood to Lwiza until the CHMT member decided to donate blood, and then told the CHMT member that blood was available to transfuse Lwiza. Also, the finding that Asha had inadequate knowledge on management of commodities could have been identified earlier. The scenario also reminds managers of health facilities of the importance of preventing frequent stockouts and overstocking to avoid expiry of medicines. The scenario alerts the managers of health facilities to strengthen monitoring and evaluation systems of health commodities.

6.3.3 Addressing the Problem and Developing an Action Plan

Using the scenario, the in-charge will assess the elements of leadership and governance that were not observed. The facility in-charge is required to conduct an investigation to determine the root causes of the problems highlighted in the scenario. The elements analyzed are transparency, accountability, equity and inclusiveness and participation.

Step 1: Addressing the Problem

(i) **Transparency**

- Acquire and document information related to the criteria used when ordering medicine and other health commodities to know whether disease burden/top ten diseases and tracer medicines were considered.
- Share with clinicians the available medicine at the facility every day.
- Share with HMT and HFGC regarding ordered and received medicines, adjustment of ordered medicine and expired medicines.
- Display all information related to the price of medicines on health facility notice boards.

(ii) **Accountability**

- Separate the roles of the storekeeper and dispenser at the health facility to ensure checks and balances.
- Conduct daily facility stock of medicines to establish the status of available medicines, determine daily consumption and monitor utilization.
- Record all medicines dispensed to exempted patients.
- Review the FFARS report to establish the percentage of funds from all sources of funding used to purchase medicines and supplies, reagents and equipment in order to ascertain whether stockouts are caused by inadequate funding.
- Conduct regular visits to the facility store and dispensing room to check the stock, arrangement of medicines, expired medicines, status of the rooms (if they are in good condition), presence of thermometers to monitor room temperature and effective utilization of medicines.
- Conduct monthly stock-taking to identify the status of health commodities that include available medicine and expiration dates.

- Orient staff on the rational use of medical equipment and other technologies.
- Ensure health commodity recording and reporting tools, such as prescriptions, ledgers, MTUHA 4/GoTHOMIS/eLMIS and bin cards are available at the facility.
- Ensure that therapeutic committee meetings are conducted as frequently as needed and documented accordingly.

(iii) **Participation**
- Ensure full participation of all members of the HFGC, HMT and therapeutics committee in meetings discussing issues related to procurement, availability and utilization of health commodities and technologies.

(iv) **Equity and inclusiveness**
- Facilitate availability of health commodities for all vulnerable groups, including pregnant women and people with disabilities; for instance, oxytocin, albino oil and hats.
- Facilitate blood availability at the facility blood bank.

Step 2: Developing an Action Plan

The health facility in-charge is required to address the identified shortfall using a plan of action that indicates the set of activities to address the problem. The plan might include the problem and its causes, the activity, the time frame and the responsible person, as indicated in Table 6.1. The in-charge should share and discuss the identified problem, possible causes and action plan with the health facility committee, health staff and the management committee for the health facility. In addition, the in-charge should monitor the results of the action plan to determine whether it leads to an improvement, and should share the results of the monitoring. The accountability mechanisms in the health facilities should be strengthened to ensure access and availability of health commodities and technologies. This will include the use of health-related guidelines and standard operating procedures, frequent management meetings, record keeping and tracking, supportive supervisions of all levels and experience sharing.

6.4 SCENARIO TWO

A pharmaceutical assistant of Mkunanzini Health Centre ordered medicines and dental equipment on February 5th, 2020, through report and request (R&R) forms. Items ordered were dental equipment, ketamine and oxytocin.

TABLE 6.1 Action Plan to Address Stockouts, Overstocking and Technical Skills at the Health Facility

PROBLEM	DESCRIPTION OF THE PROBLEM	POTENTIAL CAUSES OF THE PROBLEM	PROPOSED ACTIVITIES TO ADDRESS THE PROBLEM	RESPONSIBLE PERSON	DEADLINE FOR ADDRESSING THE PROBLEM
Stockouts of health commodities	Stockouts occurs in the health facility when there are no health commodities or technology temporarily	• Failure to plan and budget • Poor management • Poor data use	• Reporting on stock status (ordered and received, adjustment) • Reporting daily consumption of medicines • Physically verifying the availability of 10 tracers for issue to clients • Informed planning and budgeting for essential health commodities	Health facility in-charge	One week from the date the action plan was developed
Overstocking and expiry of health commodities	Overstocking occurs when there excess of required health commodities, leading to expiry	• Failure to plan • Poor management of medicine and health commodities • Failure to document and trace expiry dates • Failure to separate the expired commodities	• Reporting on expired commodities • Separating the expired commodities waiting for disposal, or removing them from the inventory • Checking if the fridge is working with a reliable power source—temperature monitoring records • Visiting the storage areas: checking if the room is secured, well ventilated, protected from heat and light, well arranged and cleaned with adequate shelves and a worktop for record keeping	Health facility in-charge	Two weeks from the date the action plan was developed

(continued)

TABLE 6.1 (Continued)

PROBLEM	DESCRIPTION OF THE PROBLEM	POTENTIAL CAUSES OF THE PROBLEM	PROPOSED ACTIVITIES TO ADDRESS THE PROBLEM	RESPONSIBLE PERSON	DEADLINE FOR ADDRESSING THE PROBLEM
Lack of technical skills	This problem occurs when the health providers do not have the required skills in procurement and supply of health commodities, as well as skills related for planning, budgeting and management of the same	• Lack of training opportunities • Limited short and refresher courses on dispensing, eLMIS, and other related skills • Failure to document skill profile and qualification	• Seeking training opportunities on eLMIS and for management of medicine and medical supplies • Updating health worker skills profile for each cadre • Documenting the qualifications of the staff at the health facility • tasks among available professionals according to task sharing, as per the policy guidelines	Health facility in-charge	Two weeks from the date the action plan was developed

However, dental equipment was out of stock; thus, the MSD advised the facility's pharmaceutical assistant to prepare a special procurement order, which would take six months before delivery.

Moreover, anesthetic drugs and oxytocin were out of stock as well, though the MSD could not give an out-of-stock notice to permit procurement from the prime vendor. Despite not having a written out-of-stock notice from the MSD, the facility pharmaceutical assistant decided to request the missing items from prime vendor; however, some of the ordered items were out of stock as well. The facility pharmaceutical assistant decided to inform the facility in-charge, who in turn requested permission from the council director through the DMO office to procure the missing items from other short-listed vendors. Council procurement officer advised council director not to honor the facility request simply because there was no written out-of-stock notice from the MSD.

The facility pharmaceutical assistant and facility in-charge decided to share the matter in their morning clinical meeting for discussion, and it was agreed that they should keep waiting until the items were available and delivered from the MSD and not otherwise, in order to avoid audit queries. Furthermore, clients kept seeking health services from Mkunanzini Health Centre without dental services and procuring missing medicines from nearby private drugs outlet at the Accredited Drug Dispensing Outlet (ADDO).

6.4.1 Consider these Questions

1. Is this scenario relevant in your health facility? How often does it happen?
2. Who is responsible for challenges experienced in the scenario and how can they be held accountable?
3. How can the challenges experienced in the scenario be addressed?

6.4.2 Reflection

The scenario portrays challenges that are sometimes beyond the capacity of the facility in-charge and HMT. The facility ordered the medicines and equipment, but the equipment was out of stock at the MSD. The out-of-stock notice was not issued by the MSD to allow the facility to procure from the prime vendor. The facility attempted to use various ways to procure the missing equipment but failed and decided to keep waiting until the items became available at the MSD to avoid audit queries. Health facilities are frequently challenged for not having essential medicine and health commodities, but the scenario expands other possible causes of stockouts to the MSD and prime vendors, who are essential in the supply chain.

6.4.3 Addressing the Problem and Developing an Action Plan

Using the indicators highlighted in the scenario, the health facility in-charge will need to evaluate the elements of leadership and governance that were not observed. Investigation to determine the root courses related to procurement challenges is important. The elements analyzed are transparency, accountability, equity and inclusiveness and participation.

Step 1: Addressing the Problem

(i) **Transparency**
   - Share the difficulties faced by the facility in the procurement of health commodities to different authorities such as the CHMT, committees, health boards and the WDC.
   - Share updates of the commodities and technologies ordered and feedback from the MSD and prime vendors to all relevant structures to know what is going on, including village leaders and the WDC.

(ii) **Accountability**
   - Make close follow-up on commodities ordered from the MSD, prime vendor and other suppliers and document all follow-ups made.
   - Consult a council procurement officer to hold tender board meetings when there is a stockout at the MSD and prime vendors. Attach all documents and written correspondences with the MSD and prime vendors.
   - Make an appointment and meet with the MSD representative to share the challenges faced in relation to the procurement of health commodities.
   - Use the status of medicine and health commodity data when ordering the same from the MSD.
   - Procured commodities should be inspected by the facility inspection committee and facility therapeutic committee before storage.

(iii) **Participation**
   - Organize meetings with all responsible facility governing structures for procuring health commodities.

Step 2: Developing an Action Plan

An action plan is developed to address the problems identified in the health facility. This is the role of the health facility in-charge. The plan of action

TABLE 6.2 Action Plan to Address Procurement Challenges at the Health Facility

PROBLEM	DESCRIPTION OF THE PROBLEM	POTENTIAL CAUSES OF THE PROBLEM	PROPOSED ACTIVITIES TO ADDRESS THE PROBLEM	RESPONSIBLE PERSON	DEADLINE OF ADDRESSING THE PROBLEM
Procurement of health commodities	Procurement of health commodities becomes a problem when the facility orders the items but does not receive them on time or in completeness and is not supported to order the same from the prime vendor. Therefore the facility lacks such medicine and health commodities.	• Late order • Lack of skills for procurement of health commodities • Failure to issue an out-of-stock notice by the MSD • Depending on only one prime vendor • Lack of networking skills • Not making enough follow-ups • Not using the existing structures when procuring commodities • Not sharing bad experiences of procuring health commodities	• Make the order on time, preferably a month or more before stockout • Frequently update procurement skills and experience sharing • Make follow-ups with the MSD and, if possible, ask to meet them to know the status of your order • Seek advice on the possibility to use more than one prime vendor • Communicate with other facilities to know how they have managed to secure health commodities • Inform the existing structures to get their support • Consult council pharmacist frequently for advice and assistance in procuring health commodities	Health facility in-charge	Two weeks from the date the action plan was developed

indicates the set of activities, including identifying the causes of the problem, the responsible individual to implement the activity and the time frame. The health facility in-charge is advised to share with the staff the action plan, discuss and agree and provide feedback on the implementation. The in-charge is also reminded to use health-related guidelines and standard operating procedures when developing the activities to avoid conflicting activities.

6.4.4 Other Potential Issues

The proposed solutions based on the scenario aim to give an overview of how the leadership of the facility can address day-to-day challenges affecting the functioning of the health facility. It is important to note that issues presented in the scenario are not exhaustive. This chapter suggests that the health facility in-charge and other HMT members should always consider other potential issues while executing their functions. Examples of other potential issues are presented in Box 6.1.

BOX 6.1   OTHER POTENTIAL ISSUES IN HEALTH COMMODITIES AND TECHNOLOGIES

1. Working with the community: Cooperate with communities to improve and maintain acceptable levels of healthcare. Conduct meetings with the community for awareness creation. Sensitize the community to the issue of blood donation and the need to donate blood.
2. Increasing health service coverage: Support community health workers by extending health coverage of the public. Ensure that enrollment in iCHF is increased.
3. Making use of available supporting structures: Have regular communication with pharmacists and do frequent consultation on the procurement of health commodities.
4. Ensuring efficient use of the vendor system: Propose to have more than one prime vendor when necessary to ensure availability of health commodities.
5. Providing collaborative healthcare: Distribute/share the medicines that are due to expiry with nearby facilities. Document and share best practices related to management health commodities and technologies.

6. Including planned preventive maintenance (PPM) for facility infrastructure and equipment in facility plans and budgets.
7. Assessing the shelf life, packaging and means of transport of the commodities procured.
8. Ensuring rational use of medicine according to standard treatment guidelines.
9. Establishing a facility pharmacy, which should have the medicines that are not available at normal facility medicine outlets.

6.5 REFERENCES

Atif, M., Malik, I., Dawoud, D., Gilani, A., Ahmed, N., & Babar, Z. U. D. (2019). Essential medicine list, policies, and the world health organization. In Z. U. D. Babar (Ed.), *Encyclopedia of pharmacy practice and clinical pharmacy* (pp. 239–249). Elsevier.

Bigdeli, M., Laing, R., Tomson, G., & Babar, Z. U. D. (2015). Medicines and universal health coverage: Challenges and opportunities. *Journal of Pharmaceutical Policy and Practice, 8*(1), 1–3.

Cameron, A., Ewen, M., Ross-Degnan, D., Ball, D., & Laing, R. (2009). Medicine prices, availability, and affordability in 36 developing and middle-income countries: A secondary analysis. *The Lancet, 373*(9659), 240–249.

Kuwawenaruwa, A., Wyss, K., Wiedenmayer, K., Metta, E., & Tediosi, F. (2020). The effects of medicines availability and stock-outs on household's utilization of healthcare services in Dodoma region, Tanzania. *Health Policy and Planning, 35*(3), 323–333.

Management Sciences for Health (MSH) (2017). *Leadership, management, and governance evidence compendium: From intuition to evidence: Why leadership, management, and governance matters for health system strengthening.*

Obare, V., Brolan, C. E., & Hill, P. S. (2014). Indicators for universal health coverage: Can Kenya comply with the proposed post-2015 monitoring recommendations? *International Journal for Equity in Health, 13*(1), 1–15.

Prinja, S., Gupta, A., Verma, R., Bahuguna, P., Kumar, D., Kaur, M., & Kumar, R. (2016). Cost of delivering health care services in public sector primary and community health centres in North India. *PloS One, 11*(8), e0160986.

Rauscher, M., Walkowiak, H., & Djara, M. B. (2018). *Leadership, management, and governance evidence compendium.*

Yadav, P. (2015). Health product supply chains in developing countries: Diagnosis of the root causes of underperformance and an agenda for reform. *Health Systems & Reform, 1*(2), 142–154. Retrieved March 17, 2018.

Health Financing and Financial Management

7

Mwandu Kini Jiyenze,
Albino Kalolo, Boniphace
Richard & Mackfallen G. Anasel

Contents

7.1 INTRODUCTION

Finance is one of the key resources that facilitate acquisitions of human and material resources for the provision of health services and social welfare at health facility and community levels. Health financing entails how financial resources are mobilized, pooled, and utilized to maintain and improve facility operations and, ultimately, improve health outcomes. Health financing is

DOI: 10.1201/9781003346821-7

linked closely with financial management (Cammack, 2007; Cashin et al., 2017). Good financial management supports health organizations in achieving their objectives (Richard & Daniel, 2001). Financial management is a process of planning, mobilizing, keeping and using financial resources effectively and efficiently to meet the needs or objectives of the organization (Borghi et al., 2006; Paramasivan, 2009; Richard & Daniel, 2001). It is regulated and guided by various policies, laws, regulations, guidelines and principles (MOHCDGEC, 2016).

To manage financial resources effectively and efficiently, health facility management team (HFMT) members perform a range of activities/functions including the following: financial planning and budgeting, mobilizing financial resources from various sources, disbursing and allocating funds for various uses, preparing financial reports, and supporting audit and risk management of funds (Kalolo et al., 2021; Kapologwe et al., 2019; Kuwawenaruwa et al., 2019; Wishnia & Goudge, 2021). In performing these functions, health facility managers experience challenges that negatively affect the provision of health services to individuals and communities overall (Fritzen, 2007). This chapter attempts to address these challenges by outlining how health facility managers can apply good practices and principles of leadership and governance to the field of health financing and financial management. The next section presents a scenario used to demonstrate how to address challenges related to finance in primary health facilities.

7.2 SCENARIO

A team of officials from the ministries (President's Office—Regional Administration and Local Government [PO-RALG] and Ministry of Health [MOH]) conducted supportive supervision (SS) of health facilities in three regions in mainland Tanzania. In one of the health centers (HCs), it was found that the quality of health services was poor. Upon visiting the pharmacy store, the team observed that critical health commodities were not available, and clients mostly were asked to buy at nearby private pharmacies. The health center had inadequate health staff, and they worked overtime to provide services. The staff were not paid their allowances, including on-call and extra duty allowances. The team was shocked by these findings and planned to use two days to review the facility budget plan and study the different sources of funds. This was in December, but the HC had not received funds from the central level. The team also assessed the National Health Insurance Fund (NHIF) source and found that no revenue was received from NHIF for more than months; the team was shocked to see that NHIF claims for the past three months were not submitted to the NHIF regional office. The team asked the council health management team (CHMT) members if they made any follow-up of this challenge, but they denied being informed by the HC management. Furthermore, there were no funds received by the facility from the improved Community Health Fund (iCHF) and the in-charge said they had tried to push claims of one month with rejections; they reported the issue to the district medical officer (DMO)'s office. In total, there were more than 400 claims kept in the box at the medical officer in charge (MOI)'s office, despite the fact that iCHF members received treatment with little satisfaction because of a lack of laboratory services and medicines.

In addition, the team found that funds generated through user fees was about 1,100,000 TZS per month from of 3200 patients who visited and were admitted to the HC. The average number of patients served per day was 110, and 40% of these qualified for exemption through exemption and waiver mechanisms; the exemption cost data were not collected. The HC did not have any billing system or electronic mechanisms for fund collection. Funds were collected by a medical attendant who had no financial background. There was limited availability of supplies like infection prevention and control (IPC) materials, utility bills were not paid for more than four months and it was found that the facility did not have a procurement plan to guide the procurement of goods and services. The bank statement of the HC had a balance of approximately 3,200,600 TZS, with which the in-charge had ordered some health commodities, payment of utilities and other facility requirements, but there was no feedback from the district executive director (DED)'s office about the stage of approval. The request was sent to the DMO office three weeks ago, and CHMT teams replied that they were still awaiting a response from the DEDs' office because there were some items that had to undergo procurement procedures in order not to violate the law.

Furthermore, the team assessment indicated that some key financial and procurement acts, regulations and guidelines were not available, and that staff had limited understanding of these documents. Review of the expenditure file indicated that some payment vouchers were missing, and some adequate payments were not supported with relevant documents. The team also found inadequate segregation of duties for staff involved in financial management and procurement, and collected funds were not deposited according to the requirements of financial regulations.

Moreover, the team reviewed the performance of the health facility governing committee and health facility management team. The team found that most of the health facility's governing committee agenda was usually to seek approval for purchasing medicines or spending money on certain activities that were not reflected in the annual plan. Many emergency meetings were conducted to seek approval of expenditures, and revenue and expenditure reports were not submitted or discussed in the meetings. In addition, recorded meeting minutes rarely showed the depth of discussion of the agenda. Resolutions from previous meetings were not documented at all. The resolutions were mixed up within the agenda, not given a timeline and, in most facilities, not discussed in subsequent meetings to track implementation. Health facility management team members had not conducted any meetings for the last six months to discuss and address health services.

7.2.1 Consider these Questions

1. What revenue management challenges are presented in this scenario?
2. Do the revenue management challenges identified in this scenario apply to your organization or health facilities?
3. Why do revenue management challenges exist in your health facilities?
4. Why do health facility management teams:
   a) Make payments out of plan?
   b) Fail to properly seek proper authorization?
   c) Fail to properly keep payment vouchers and related documents?
5. What procurement challenges are presented in the scenario, and why do these procurement challenges exist in this health facility?
6. Why do health facility committees not discuss revenue and expenditure reports adequately? Why do health facility committees conduct emergency meetings for approving expenditure related to procurement?
7. Why does inadequate understanding of key financial policies, laws, regulations and guidelines exist among health staff?
8. What can be done to address the financial challenges reported in this scenario?

7.2.2 Reflection

The aforementioned scenario demonstrates that health facility management faces a number of challenges related to health financing and financial management. These challenges are reported in the annual reports of the control and auditor general, and they fall under four themes as follows:

(i) **Revenue management challenges**
   - Missing revenue earning receipt books.
   - Failure to adequately collect revenue from various sources.
   - Failure to monitor revenue collection.

(ii) **Cash management challenges**
   - Bank reconciliation is not done on a monthly basis.
   - A surprise cash survey is not conducted.

(iii) **Expenditure management challenges**
   - Funds used for fruitless expenditure; unnecessary expenditure due to inadequate financial management and controls.
   - Payments for unbudgeted activities.
   - Inadequately supported expenditures.
   - Missing payment vouchers.
   - Missing acknowledgment receipts from recipients of funds.
   - Expenditure charged to wrong account codes.
   - Payments not subjected to pre-audit.
   - Lack of proper authorization of expenditure.
   - Expenditure incurred contrary to financial and planning guidelines.
   - Outstanding claims not paid.

(iv) **Procurement challenges**
   - Procurements made outside of annual procurement plans.
   - Procurement of goods and services without tender board approval.
   - Procurements made without raising a local purchase order (LPO).
   - Procurement of services from unapproved suppliers.
   - Payment for goods and services not delivered or rendered.
   - Procurements made without competitive bidding.
   - Stores/supplies not recorded in ledgers.
   - Inadequate documentation of contracts and projects.

The scenario presented just some of the financial challenges that health facility in-charges and other health facility management (HFMT) team members face. The challenges reported in the scenario include absence of billing and electronic mechanisms for fund collection, delays in submitting and making follow-ups on claims at NHIF and non-compliance with financial and procurement procedures and regulations. These are some of the indicators of weak leadership and governance at the health facility. These challenges could have been avoided if the health facility in-charge was using good practices and principles of management, leadership and governance.

7.2.3 Addressing the Problem and Developing an Action Plan

Using the aforementioned challenges, the in-charge has to assess the use of principles of leadership and governance at his or her health facility. Specifically, the facility in-charge is required to assess the root causes of the problems related to health financing and financial management. These challenges can be addressed by using good practices and principles of management, leadership and governance in the field of health financing and financial management. The good practices and principles are presented herewith under the themes of accountability, inclusiveness and participation, transparency, rule of law and equity. To address the challenges reported in the scenario, health managers can use the principles of management, leadership and governance as follows. For each principle, the specific practices or actions are listed.

Step 1: Addressing the Problem

(i) **Accountability**
- Establish/create new sources for generating revenue for the health services.
- Choose specific areas/sites for collection of revenue.
- Establish/create new sources of funding/financing mechanisms.
- Identify and closely monitor revenue from various sources.
- Properly fill and submit timely claims to various insurance schemes.
- Follow up on all insurance claims so that they are paid on time.
- Properly keep revenue books in safe and secure places.
- Issue receipts for all received money in the health facility.
- Deposit collected revenues from all sources in an appropriate bank account in a timely manner.
- Appoint a financial focal person who will ensure proper filling of NHIF/CHF forms and claims.
- Conduct bank reconciliation on a monthly basis.
- Seek approval from relevant authorities to use imprest at health facilities for emergency purposes.

- Prepare quarterly technical and financial reports and submit them to relevant authorities on time.
- Conduct surprise cash surveys.
- Prepare an appropriate health facility plan covering key services and activities.
- Approve expenditure for items and activities in the budget and compare expenditure against budget.
- Support each expense with relevant attachments/documents.
- Properly keep payment vouchers and related documents in a safe and secure place.
- All actions by staff should be supervised by appropriate people and officials.
- Budget and allocate funds for payment of staff allowances and other benefits.
- Conduct regular continuing education on financial management.
- Properly adhere to procedures and principles outlined in financial policies, laws, regulations and guidelines.
- Prepare a health facility annual plan and procurement plan.
- Purchase goods and services in line with the health facility procurement plan.
- Procure services and goods from approved suppliers using appropriate procurement methods.
- Record all goods received in a store ledger.
- Maintain/keep key documents and contracts related to procurement.
- Establish a team that will respond to queries raised by auditors.

(ii) **Participation and inclusiveness**

- Present and allow members of the health facilities committee, facility management team and staff to discuss revenue and expenditure reports.
- Present and allow members of the health facilities committee, facility management team and staff to discuss implementation of the health facility procurement plan.
- Present and allow members of the health facilities committee to discuss the implementation of the health facility procurement plan.
- Seek approval of the health facility procurement plan from the health facility committee.
- Conduct health facility management meetings on a monthly basis.
- Discuss any increase or decrease in revenue and reasons for the same with HFMT.

(iii) **Transparency**
- Seek authorization for procurement from relevant authorities.
- Present revenue and expenditure to the HFGC, HFMT and staff.

(iv) **Rule of law**
- Obtain and use key financial policies, laws, regulations and guidelines.
- Orient or train health staff on key financial policies, laws, regulations and guidelines.
- Purchase goods and services according to the public procurement act and its regulations.
- Manage and monitor exemptions at health facilities in line with national health policies and guidelines.
- Follow procedures for receiving goods from tenderers/suppliers outlined in financial policies, laws, regulations and guidelines.

(v) **Equity**
- Create community and household awareness of joining health insurance plans.
- Identify exempted individuals with insurance cards to use the cards to pay for health services.
- Assign staff to monitor exemption and waiver processes/mechanisms; record exemption and waiver costs.

Step 2: Developing an Action Plan

The in-charge is required to address the identified challenges by developing an action plan that indicates a set of activities to address identified problems. The plan should indicate the activities, time frame, and responsible person, as indicated in Table 7.1. The in-charge should share and discuss the identified problems and proposed action plan with the health facility governing committee, health staff and the management team of the health facility. In addition, the in-charge should monitor the results of the action plan to determine whether it is leading to the expected improvement, and should share the results of the monitoring. A sample action plan is prepared (see Table 7.1) to address some of the challenges reported in the scenario.

TABLE 7.1 Action Plan to Address Challenges Related to Health Financing and Financial Management

PROBLEM	DESCRIPTION OF THE PROBLEM	POTENTIAL CAUSES OF THE PROBLEM	PROPOSED ACTIVITIES TO ADDRESS THE PROBLEM	RESPONSIBLE PERSON	DEADLINE OF ADDRESSING THE PROBLEM
Allowances not paid	The health staff work beyond normal working hours, but they are not paid their entitlements/ allowances.	• Lack of budgeting • Shortage of funds	• Include on-call and other allowances in the facility plan and budget • Prepare on-call allowances and extra duties payments	Health facility in-charge	One week after the preparation of the action plan
Delayed claims submission to the NHIF	The health facility offered services through the NHIF but did not submit the claim for payments.	• Reluctance • Lack of skills to fill the claim forms • Frequent deductions from the NHIF, which discouraged the staff to fill the forms	• Prepare and submit monthly claims to the NHIF and iCHF regional offices • Orient staff on filling out NHIF forms • Seek clarification on deductions from the NHIF • Share feedback to staff on errors noted in submitted forms	Health facility in-charge	Monthly
Absence of procurement plans	The facility had no procurement plan to guide procurement of goods and services.	• Lack of planning • Lack of awareness • Lack of relevant skills	• Prepare and seek approval of the procurement plan to guide procurement of goods and services in the facility • Seek technical support from CHMT members	Facility in-charge	By next month

(continued)

TABLE 7.1 (Continued)

PROBLEM	DESCRIPTION OF THE PROBLEM	POTENTIAL CAUSES OF THE PROBLEM	PROPOSED ACTIVITIES TO ADDRESS THE PROBLEM	RESPONSIBLE PERSON	DEADLINE OF ADDRESSING THE PROBLEM
Limited understanding of financial and procurement acts and regulations	Staff were lacking basic knowledge on financial and procurement management	• Absence of acts and regulations at facility • Lack of knowledge and skill	• Communicate with relevant authorities to determine the missing guidelines • Orient health facility staff on health financing and financial management	Health facility in-change	Immediately
Poor management of exemptions and waivers	Exemptions and waivers were not monitored, and there was no data/information for exempted people	• Limited knowledge on how to manage exemptions and waivers	• Appoint a staff member to manage exemptions and waivers • Orient the staff on how to handle exemptions and waivers	Health facility in-charge	Immediately
Poor participation of decision-making bodies or structures	Members of the health facilities governing committee did not discuss revenue and expenditure reports	• Health facilities governing committee not knowing their roles	Orient health facility governing committee members on roles in financial management	Health facility in-charge	Immediately

7.3 REFERENCES

Borghi, J. O., Ensor, T., Somanathan, A., Lissner, C., Mills, A., & Lancet Maternal Survival Steering Group (2006). Mobilising financial resources for maternal health. *The Lancet, 368*(9545), 1457–1465.

Cammack, J. (2007). *Building capacity through financial management: A practical guide*. Oxfam GB.

Cashin, C., Bloom, D., Sparkes, S., Barroy, H., Kutzin, J., O'Dougherty, S., & World Health Organization (2017). *Aligning public financial management and health financing: Sustaining progress toward universal health coverage*. Issue WHO/HIS/HGF/HFWorking Paper/17.4. World Health Organization.

Fritzen, S. A. (2007). Strategic management of the health workforce in developing countries: What have we learned? *Human Resources for Health, 5*(1), 1–9

Kalolo, A., Kapologwe, N. A., Samky, H., & Kibusi, S. M. (2021). Acceptability of the direct health facility financing (DHFF) initiative in Tanzania: A mixed methods process evaluation of the moderating factors. *The International Journal of Health Planning and Management*. https://doi.org/10.1002/hpm.3402

Kapologwe, N. A., Kalolo, A., Kibusi, S. M., Chaula, Z., Nswilla, A., Teuscher, T., Aung, K., & Borghi, J. (2019). Understanding the implementation of direct health facility financing and its effect on health system performance in Tanzania: A non-controlled before and after mixed method study protocol. *Health Research Policy and Systems, 17*(1), 11. https://doi.org/10.1186/s12961-018-0400-3

Kuwawenaruwa, A., Remme, M., Mtei, G., Makawia, S., Maluka, S., Kapologwe, N., & Borghi, J. (2019). Bank accounts for public primary health care facilities: Reflections on implementation from three districts in Tanzania. *The International Journal of Health Planning and Management, 34*(1), e860–e874. https://doi.org/10.1002/hpm.2702

MOHCDGEC (2016). *Guideline for developing annual health centre and dispensary plans*. Ministry of Health, Community Development, Gender, Elderly and Children and President's Office—Regional Administration and Local Government.

Paramasivan, C. (2009). *Financial management*. New Age International.

Richard, A., & Daniel, T. (Eds.). (2001). *Managing public expenditure, a reference book for transition countries: A reference book for transition countries*. OECD Publishing.

Wishnia, J., & Goudge, J. (2021). Strengthening public financial management in the health sector: A qualitative case study from South Africa. *BMJ Global Health, 6*(11), e006911. https://doi.org/10.1136/bmjgh-2021-006911

Community Health Systems Management and Governance

8

Ntuli A. Kapologwe, Albino Kalolo,
James Kengia, Idda Lyatonga Swai,
Anosisye Mwandulusya Kesale,
Godfrey Kacholi, Mwandu Kini
Jiyenze & Mackfallen G. Anasel

Contents

DOI: 10.1201/9781003346821-8

8.1 INTRODUCTION

A community health system is a combination of local actors, their relationships and their processes in producing, advocating and supporting health in communities and households, beyond but in relation to the formal health system structures (Schneider et al., 2022; Schneider & Lehmann, 2016). As a social system, a community health system is characterized by both hierarchical and horizontal elements based on networking and relying on trust and acceptability (Sacks et al., 2019; Schneider, 2019). Its management involves making use of the existing local actors and their relationships to ensure that activities and processes are well planned, organized, coordinated and controlled in an effort to improve community health. This involves the effective use of a human workforce and materials in healthcare settings and ensures that each actor is aware of their roles and responsibilities in attaining desired goals.

Over the years, Tanzania has embraced community healthcare as a part of the healthcare system and has made several improvements. Notable efforts to improve community health systems can be traced back to the Arusha declaration (1967), which put forward a clear policy of expanding primary healthcare services at the grassroots level by constructing health facilities and training village health workers to conduct community outreach (Bech et al., 2013; Dominicus & Akamatsu, 1989). In the early 2010s, the Community-Based Health Program (CBHP) was formulated to address the lack of coordination, standardization, monitoring, supervision and support across a range of community health programs operating at the local level (Shelley et al., 2020). In 2014, the government formulated the National Community-Based Care Policy Guidelines and established the National Community-Based Health Programme (NCBHP) in the Health Promotion section of the Ministry of Health (MOH) to oversee the implementation (Brown, 2018). The Community-Based Health Policy 2014 officially recognized and standardized community health worker (CHW) cadres and the services that they deliver, as reflected in the 2013 National Essential Health Care Interventions Package—Tanzania (NEHCIP). In early 2020, the 2014 National Community-Based Health Program Policy Guideline was replaced by the Policy Guidelines for Community-Based Health and Social Welfare Services, which was made to address the challenges of the earlier version. In these new guidelines, the government focused on locally grown solutions that could be implemented by the community without external sources. These new guidelines re-introduce the use of volunteer CHWs nationwide. The newly proposed approach is based on the success of the Uturo community in the Mbarali district, Mbeya region, which used community volunteers to address issues of maternal and newborn deaths successfully, famously known as the Uturo Model (Kanjanja, 2021).

The 2020 Policy Guidelines also provide a governance framework for implementing CBHC services that includes elaborating the systems and structures for organization, management and coordination, and assigning roles and responsibilities for each level. The guidelines provide a framework for partnership, collaboration and coordination for all stakeholders including the government, development partners and private sector.

The MOH oversees the CBHP, while the PO-RALG is chiefly responsible for its implementation. Non-governmental organizations (NGOs), donors and other partners support CBHP planning and implementation at all levels, including goal- and objective-setting, resource mobilization and information-sharing.

Making community systems work also depends on how the community is engaged. Community engagement (also known as community participation or community involvement) is a process concerned with raising awareness, with the ultimate involvement of individuals, families and communities in the planning, implementation and control of activities geared towards improving health and general welfare through self-reliance (Chaskin, 2001; King & Cruickshank, 2012). It also refers to voluntary involvement of the public or community members in activities that affect them, that is, identification of a problem, planning, implementation and providing resources to find the solution up to the point of evaluation by the community, which means the community manages the process (Christophe & Neiland, 2006; Zakus & Lysack, 1998). The process of community involvement involves an exchange of information leading to action by the people to improve a situation for a better life. In health facility management, community engagement at different levels is crucial. In Tanzania's situation, various formal and informal structures are available to promote community engagement; these structures and responsibilities are listed in Table 8.1.

TABLE 8.1   Formal and Informal Structures for Promoting Community Engagement

STRUCTURES	ROLES/RESPONSIBILITIES
Village council	Making overall planning decisions on and giving support for health service delivery
Village health committees	Making planning decisions and giving support for health service delivery, assessing health services and making suggestions for suitable improvements

(continued)

TABLE 8.1   *(Continued)*

STRUCTURES	ROLES/RESPONSIBILITIES
Health facility governance board and committees	Overseeing health service planning, service delivery, and management of health resources, and monitoring and evaluating health services at the facility
Council health service board	Overseeing service delivery and management of health resources in the councils
Community-based groups	Forming organized groups of individuals in the community with a shared goal mostly related to economic empowerment or helping each other during sickness or funeral arrangement for a group member or close relative; e.g. VIKOBA
Influential community leaders (such as religious or tribal leaders such as Maasai laibons)	Leading and coordinating the society or group of people in maintaining the practices of particular agreed-upon societal norms, standards, beliefs or culture; highly respected member of the respective community

8.2 SCENARIO ONE

The government of Tanzania has approved resources for upgrading one of the dispensaries in "Ward X" to become a health center. "Ward X" is inhabited by a society that is patriarchal in nature, with the elders deciding most matters for the society. The district executive director (DED) has dispatched a technical team to assess potential areas where the project could be executed. On arrival at the ward, the team, in consultation with the ward executive officer (WEO), managed to find a dispensary, "dispensary Y", deemed potentially suitable from technical expertise to be upgraded to function as a health center. A report was written and given to the DED, who approved the commencement of the project and appointed the health facility in-charge of dispensary Y to oversee the project implementation. Upon commencement of the project, there was reluctance of the community to participate in the site clearance, bringing construction materials available for free from nearby river banks (construction sand and stones). The project execution was therefore not possible given the prerequisite of utilizing the approved fund that some of the works must be handled by the community members in order to minimize the project cost.

8.2.1 Consider these Questions

1. What are the lessons learned in this situation with regard to the importance of community engagement?
2. Has your organization/health facility ever experienced a similar situation (or have you heard from another facility/organization)?
3. What could be the possible causes of problems evolved in this project?
4. Could these problems be avoided?

8.2.2 Addressing the Problem and Developing an Action Plan

This situation serves as an example of the importance of appropriate community engagement in the management of projects for healthcare organizations. Project execution in the community needs the engagement of both technical and community members from the conceptual phase of the project. Despite the fact that the WEO was engaged during the conceptual phase of the project, the community or community representatives were not engaged fully in the site selection, and were also informed about the project financing models and the roles of the community during the project implementation. In this situation, the roles of elders in society, though not in the formal structure, need to be appreciated due to the fact that they play a vital role in enhancing community participation.

Step 1: Addressing the Problem

In this scenario, the governance and leadership issues in the project execution relate to participation, transparency and accountability. To address these aspects of governance and leadership, the in-charges should address the following issues:

(i) **Participation:** In order to create community engagement and project ownership, it is important for the facility in-charge to systematically understand key influential individuals in the society and also to engage the leaders in the formal structure. This can be achieved by:
   - Stakeholder mapping and understanding the power relationship in the community.

- Organizing and conducting stakeholder meetings that include participants such as community leaders from formal or informal structures (highly respected or influential members of the society/religious leaders and civil society organizations.
- Presenting the project idea in community structure meetings (village general assembly and ward development committee).

(ii) **Transparency:** The facility in-charge needs to
- share information widely related to the project with all key stakeholders.
- provide customized information to all key stakeholders showing the project benefit to them.

(iii) **Accountability:** The facility in-charge needs to
- address people's concerns within his/her scope and provide clarifications whenever needed.
- monitor, inform and continuously engage informal influential community leaders in the society.
- organize regular meetings for project updates with key community stakeholders.

Step 2: Developing an Action Plan

An action plan is developed to address the problems identified in the execution of a project at the health facility. This is the role of the health facility in-charge. The plan of action indicates the set of activities, including identifying the causes of the problem, the responsible person to implement the activity and the time frame. The in-charge should share and discuss the identified problem, possible causes and solutions with the health facility governing committee and health facility management teams. In addition, the in-charge should monitor implementation of the action plan to know whether they lead to an improvement. The results of the monitoring should be shared with the health facility governing committee and health facility management teams.

8.3 SCENARIO TWO

The residents of Kisajanilo village have been experiencing serious health issues, particularly those related to epidemic diseases such as malaria and diarrhea. The volume of people seeking medical care overwhelms the existing health infrastructure, that is, the local public dispensary. The dispensary

TABLE 8.2 Action Plan to Address Community Engagement Challenges at the Health Facility

PROBLEM	DESCRIPTION OF THE PROBLEM	POTENTIAL CAUSES OF THE PROBLEM	PROPOSED ACTIVITIES TO ADDRESS THE PROBLEM	RESPONSIBLE PERSON	DEADLINE FOR ADDRESSING THE PROBLEM
Inadequate engagement of the community	Inability of the project team lead to identify the potential influential leaders in the community and engage with the formal community structures resulted in inadequate awareness and motivation of the community to contribute to the project execution. This ultimately resulted in delays in the project implementation.	• Inadequate stakeholder mapping to understand key players • Inadequate information sharing with the community • Low community awareness of the project • Inadequate understanding of the potential of influential community leaders	• Mapping of key stakeholders • Conduct meetings with community members by utilizing existing formal structures • Identify and engage influential community leaders	Health facility in-charge	Two weeks from the date action plan was developed

is understaffed, as it has only three health workers who work for more than eleven hours a day. Because the facility health workers are busy attending to community residents at the village dispensary, HIV patients have ceased receiving treatment from the local PLHIV group, and no one was available to reconnect them to the PLHIV center. Everyone in the village assembly, including the village elders, blames the dispensary staff for not being in charge of the general welfare of the community. One woman, who is a member of the community, volunteered to provide some basic community health services, such as promoting nutrition services to children under the age of five. She only attended a one-time training five years ago. One NGO operating in the ward asked community health workers to attend a four-day workshop on infectious diseases in their ward last year. All attendees were offered a travel reimbursement and five per diems as compensation. Although it was addressed to the village chairperson, the invitation letter reached out to the village dispensary. The village chairperson decided that his wife, who has never volunteered for anything related to community health, should attend the workshop after learning that attendees will receive per diems. Even after returning from the training village, the chairperson's wife never bothered to deal with COVID-19 or anything else related to infectious diseases. The facility in-charge has come under fire from the village health committees and other stakeholders for not choosing the individual who has been helping the village's efforts to promote community health. The village chairman and his wife have promised that they would not be re-elected in the upcoming election, which has angered the locals. Despite the three staff members' devotion to save the entire village, the facility manager is demotivated by the opinion of the village government and the community that the village dispensary health workers are no longer beneficial to the community.

8.3.1 Consider these Questions

1. What lesson have you learnt from this scenario regarding the use of community health workers (CHWs)?
2. Has your health facility or work setting ever encountered common challenges regarding the management of CHWs?
3. What is another challenge facing community health that you think could be addressed through good coordination and management of CHWs?
4. What do you think are the causes of these problems?
5. Do you think that the health facility in-charge and facility management team play a big role in making CHW play an active role in providing community health services?

8.3.2 Reflection

The scenario provided represents many other common challenges facing the community health system in Tanzania and beyond. Many health facilities are understaffed but have not recognized the importance of using CHWs to complement their roles. Community health can be addressed by using community members, known as CHWs, if well-coordinated and incentivized. However, in many areas, this has not been successfully done. The responsible organs for influencing the use and management of the CHW are disconnected and not showing up, and the community members who are willing to take responsibility of serving their fellow community members are not supported effectively, making them vulnerable in these situations.

8.3.3 Addressing the Problem and Developing an Action Plan

Step 1: Addressing the Problem

(i) **Participation**
- Engage CHWs in the development of facility plans.
- Engage CHWs in provision promotion services, such as vaccination and sensitization activities.
- Engage the village or ward government in discussing the roles that will be assigned to CHWs in the community.

(ii) **Accountability**
- Link CHWs with community health stakeholders in your areas.
- Prepare interventions that will help to build the capacity of the CHW.
- Help the community to identify the CHW with whom they are willing to work.
- Help the village government/ward to follow the selection procedure of getting CHWs in the community.
- If possible, provide working tools to the CHWs.

(iii) **Transparency**
- Share health challenges with community health stakeholders such as CHWs and the village government.
- Share the health interventions with CHW that the facility plans implement in the community.
- Communicate reports and feedback regarding community health services to the CHWs, village governments and other stakeholders.

Step 2: Developing an Action Plan

TABLE 8.3   An Action Plan for Addressing Community-Related Challenges

PROBLEM	DESCRIPTION OF THE PROBLEM	POTENTIAL CAUSES OF THE PROBLEM	PROPOSED ACTIVITIES TO ADDRESS THE PROBLEM	RESPONSIBLE PERSON	DEADLINE FOR ADDRESSING THE PROBLEM
Inadequate management of CHWs in the illage	Failure of the village governance structures and health facility management team to coordinate community engagement in health promotion through the use of CHWs	• Lack of communication between the village leaders and health facility in-charge	Establish a strong linkage between village governments and health facilities	Health facility in-charge	Within three weeks of developing the action plan
		• Lack of awareness of the formal structures for selecting CHWs	Build awareness of the formal/village structures and their roles to CHWs	Health facility in-charge	Four weeks after developing the action plan
		• Uncoordinated management of CHWs	Coordinate the functions of CHWs, community and formal structures through village government	Village government leaders and Health Facility in charges	Four weeks after developing the action plan
		• Failure to link CWHs and stakeholders for capacity-building activities	Link CHWs with health stakeholders	Health facility in-charge and village government leaders	Two weeks after developing the plan
		• Inadequate capacity of CHWs in addressing community health	Build capacity of CHWs regarding their roles and responsibilities	Health facility in-charge	Six weeks after development of the action plan

8.4 SCENARIO THREE

Somoye, a married, pregnant woman with two children, didn't go to school because she was married at age of 15 years. Her family economy depends on small-scale farming (subsistence) in a village. The village has strong traditions and beliefs that a twin pregnancy is a curse. The village has no health facility, and the closest is about 7 km from her home. In her third pregnancy, she attended the antenatal clinic (ANC) twice but wasn't told if she had a twin pregnancy. As she had two deliveries at home assisted by a traditional birth attendant, she expected things will be the same in her third delivery. As the final days of her pregnancy were approaching, she found that she had started labor pain before the expected dates that appeared on her ANC card. She asked the traditional birth attendants to support her, and they came to support her. No one knew that she had twin pregnancy, not even herself. After some hours of labor, she finally had her baby without any difficulty, a few minutes later they had a second twin, and the birth attendants were shocked that she had a twin pregnancy. The mother and her twins were left without any support, as her husband was travelling, and her 6-year-old daughter was the only help she could get.

She noticed a small amount of bleeding began a few hours after the delivery and was increasing as time went by, but she had nothing to do as she was not able to walk to the dispensary 7 km away from home. She tried to call her brother from the next village by sending someone, as there was no network for mobile phone communication.

Her brother arrived the next morning she found her unconscious with blood around her bed; he decided to carry her on his back and one twin baby. The second baby was carried by the daughter, and they started walking to the dispensary; they walked down to the mountainous village for five hours. They were quickly received and after a few minutes, she died, and the twins babies were also admitted. They could not take the body back home due to her situation of having twins, so she was buried near the dispensary.

8.4.1 Consider these Questions

1. What are the key leadership and governance challenges experienced in this community?
2. Does your community experience similar challenges?
3. Which stakeholders can be involved to address these challenges?

8.4.2 Reflection

This scenario reminds the health facility in-charge and the health facility management team members of the role of cultural belief systems in influencing community health-seeking behaviors. Health facility managers should be able to scan cultural beliefs and practices that act as stumbling blocks for health-seeking behavior and in maintaining a healthy community. The health facility managers should work with the community actors, such as community leaders, influential persons, community resource persons (such as community health workers, cultural organizations and women's groups) and civil society organizations, to promote health and move away from practices that do not promote health. Moreover, the fact that the healthcare workers could not diagnose multiple pregnancies highlights the poor quality of services, which could have already saved this life. The consequences of poor-quality health services do not only end with the patient that is attended but affects the whole community. She could not have fallen into traditional birth attendants whose beliefs were not favorable to save her life. In addition, the topics on health education provided in antenatal care could have been customized to local needs (topics driven by local problems) in order to address such strong beliefs and cultural taboos that have devastating consequences on community health.

This scenario points out leadership and management problems manifested as community participation, quality of care and equity and social justice. Moreover, the fact that this lady was abandoned by everyone except her close relatives points to a lack of transparency, accountability and communication between the health facility and community leadership structures.

8.4.3 Addressing the Problem and Developing an Action Plan

Step 1: Addressing the Problem

In this scenario, the governance and leadership issues in health service delivery presented relate to participation, transparency, accountability, equity and social justice and quality of health services. To address these aspects of governance and leadership, the in-charges should:

(i) **Participation:**
  • Create community partnerships that can tackle community problems with their roots in community beliefs, taboos and value systems. This can be achieved by:

- holding multi-stakeholder meetings that include such participants as community leaders, influential persons and civil society organizations.
- presenting such issues in community structure meetings such as village/Mtaa council meetings, Mtaa/village general assembly.
- creating community-based campaigns on cultural practices that influence health.

(ii) **Transparency:**
- Create a forum where community leaders will transparently share community-related issues that need to be addressed in order to improve community health.
- Present community-related challenges in village/Mtaa structure meetings and allow open discussion and make transparent resolutions on the actions.

(iii) **Accountability:**
- Prepare guidelines on the scope of work of traditional birth attendants and other community resource persons, such as community health workers.

(iv) **Equity and social justice**
- Ensure screening of community members who have vulnerable situations as they come for healthcare and work with the community to jointly look for solutions.
- Identify community-based issues that create inequities and socially unjust acts and present them in village/Mtaa meetings for joint solutions.

(v) **Quality of services**
- Ensure that quality antenatal services are provided in the health facility through continuous quality improvement audits.
- Check whether health education sessions at the antenatal clinic address community-related challenges and emanate from challenges encountered in routine practices at the clinic and community outreaches.
- Monitor routine feedback on the quality of services as received from health facility sources, community-related meetings or other sources.

Step 2: Developing an Action Plan

TABLE 8.4 An Action Plan for Addressing Community-Related Challenges

PROBLEM	DESCRIPTION OF THE PROBLEM	POTENTIAL CAUSES OF THE PROBLEM	PROPOSED ACTIVITIES TO ADDRESS THE PROBLEM	RESPONSIBLE PERSON	DEADLINE FOR ADDRESSING THE PROBLEM
Poor accessibility to health services	The mother had to travel 7 km to reach the health facility.	• Lack of joint community actions to address the issue of distance from health facilities • Lack of leadership to address the challenges related to transport and communication • Lack of reliable transport to the health facility • Absence of q mobile phone network for easy communication	• Discuss with the community the need to construct a health facility in the village or address transport issues by having a community-based transport (funds for transport) system that is available for emergencies • Include in the health facility budget the issues of transport/ambulance	Facility in-charge	Within a month of developing the action plan
Teenage pregnancies and early marriages	The mother has a history of being married at early age.	• Lack of education • Traditional norms of early marriages	• Present the issue in village/ward committee meetings • Develop action plans for promoting youth-friendly services in health facilities and community outreach in order to reach many young people	Facility in-charge	Within a month of developing the action plan

Persistent cultural taboos that influence health-seeking behavior	The traditional birth attendants and the entire community left the mother and babies dying because of twin pregnancy.	• No community-based campaigns to address bad cultural taboos • Health education at the antenatal clinic does not address community health issues • Traditional birth attendants lack guidelines on how to address cultural issues and attend clients ethically	• Create community-based campaigns to address community-based taboos • Present the case in village/Mtaa meetings for joint action • Prepare guidelines and scope of work of community resource persons such as traditional birth attendants and community health workers	Facility in-charge	Within a week of developing the action plan
Poor quality of antenatal care	Failure to detect a multiple pregnancy.	• Poor skills of healthcare workers to diagnose multiple pregnancy/danger signs	• Train health workers on basic and comprehensive antenatal care • Conduct mentorship and supportive supervision	District Medical officer	Within six months after developing the plan

8.5 REFERENCES

Bech, M. M., Lawi, Y. Q., Massay, D. A., & Rekdal, O. B. (2013). Changing policies and their influence on government health workers in Tanzania, 1967–2009: Perspectives from rural Mbulu district. *The International Journal of African Historical Studies, 46*(1), 61–103.

Brown, L. E. (2018). *Applying stated-preference methods to health systems problems in sub-Saharan Africa.* Johns Hopkins University.

Chaskin, R. J. (2001). Building community capacity: A definitional framework and case studies from a comprehensive community initiative. *Urban Affairs Review, 36*(3), 291–323.

Christophe, B., & Neiland, A. (2006). *From participation to governance: A critical review of the concepts of governance, co-management and participation, and their implementation in small-scale inland fisheries in developing countries.* A Review Prepared for the Challenge Program on Water and Food. The World Fish Centre and the CGIAR Challenge Program on Water and Food.

Dominicus, D. A., & Akamatsu, T. (1989). Health policy and implementations in Tanzania. *The Keio Journal of Medicine, 38*(2), 192–200.

Kanjanja, E. M. (2021). *Evaluation of a community-based maternal and child health initiative of Uturo village in Mbarali district and prospects to scale-up the initiative in Tanzania.* Muhimbili University of Health and Allied Sciences.

King, C., & Cruickshank, M. (2012). Building capacity to engage: Community engagement or government engagement? *Community Development Journal, 47*(1), 5–28.

Sacks, E., Morrow, M., Story, W. T., Shelley, K. D., Shanklin, D., Rahimtoola, M., Rosales, A., Ibe, O., & Sarriot, E. (2019). Beyond the building blocks: Integrating community roles into health systems frameworks to achieve health for all. *BMJ Global Health, 3*(Suppl 3), e001384. https://doi.org/10.1136/bmjgh-2018-001384

Schneider, H. (2019). The governance of national community health worker programmes in low-and middle-income countries: An empirically based framework of governance principles, purposes and tasks. *International Journal of Health Policy and Management, 8*(1), 18.

Schneider, H., & Lehmann, U. (2016). From community health workers to community health systems: Time to widen the horizon? *Health Systems and Reform, 2*(2), 112–118. https://doi.org/10.1080/23288604.2016.1166307

Schneider, H., Olivier, J., Orgill, M., Brady, L., Whyle, E., Zulu, J., San Sebastian, M., George, A., & The Chaminuka Collective (2022). The multiple lenses on the community health system: Implications for policy, practice and research. *International Journal of Health Policy and Management, 11*(1), 9.

Shelley, K. D., Frumence, G., & Kasangala, A. (2020). Tanzania's community-based health program. *Health for the People: National Community Health Worker Programs from Afghanistan to Zimbabwe, 381.*

Zakus, J. D. L., & Lysack, C. L. (1998). Revisiting community participation. *Health Policy and Planning, 13*(1), 1–12.

Index

Note: Page numbers in **bold** indicate a table.

Printed in the United States
by Baker & Taylor Publisher Services